D1668903

PHEKARUMA TRAVEL GUIDES

In collaboration with

 tredition

ROTHENBURG OB DER TAUBER

STRICTLY CONFIDENTIAL

PHEKARUMA TRAVEL GUIDE

RUDOLF H. STEHLE

Copyright © Rudolf H. Stehle, PhD

ISBN Softcover: 978-3-384-17583-0
ISBN Hardcover: 978-3-384-17584-7

First published 2024

Photo Credits
All photos were taken be Rudolf H. Stehle, PhD in HDR Qualität.

Disclaimer
The information provided within this book is for general informational purposes only. Although the author has made every effort to ensure that the information in this book is correct, there are no representations or warranties, express or implied, about the completeness, accuracy, reliability, suitability or availability with respect to the information or related graphics contained in this book for any purpose. The author does not assume and hereby disclaim any liability to any party for any loss, damage, or disruption caused by errors or omissions, whether such errors or omissions result from negligence, accident, or any other cause. Any use of this information is at your own risk.

◄ **Cover Page:** The Plönlein in the neighbourhood Kappenzipfel.

► **Rear Cover:** The town hall at the Marktplatz, the central square.

Preface

Rothenburg ob der Tauber is not just a city but a living being with a thrilling story. Its heroes have woven their deeds into the fabric of history, creating a tapestry of culture and customs that is as fascinating as it is unique. While every society rests on opposites, the way Rothenburg has dealt with conflict sets it apart. Rather than letting history become tragic, Rothenburg has embraced new ideas and challenged the past, creating a dynamic and ever-evolving town that is a pleasure to delve into.

The guide *Rothenburg ob der Tauber: Strictly Confidential* seeks to unveil the historically grown network of this incredible town, making its dynamic visible to all who seek to write their own story. As one explores Rothenburg's winding streets and charming architecture, one will discover the mark each period of history has left on the town's morphology. It's a joy to gain insight into Rothenburg's rich history, and it is even more a pleasure to share it with others.

Subjective experience is always specific, and your story of Rothenburg will be different from mine. But that's the beauty of this world - it inspires us to write our own story, to embrace meaningful subjectivity, and to counterbalance with experience our blind faith in objective truth based on facts and figures. So come and explore Rothenburg ob der Tauber - feel inspired to create your thrilling chapter in this incredible journey through time.

Rudolf H. Stehle

Content

Introduction 1

A first Glance at Rothenburg ob der Tauber 1

Rothenburg's History 5

Chronicles of Rothenburg 10

Theme Parks and Adventure Tours 14

Travel Points at a Glance 16

Culinary Delights 20

Annual Calendar 22

Highlight Tour 1: Old Town 24

Highlight Tour 2: Burggarten 26

Highlight Tour 3: Tauber Valley 28

Walkabouts 30

The Magic of Rothenburg 31

Rothenburg's Old Town 32

(1) Marktplatz 36

(2) Town Hall 38

(3) Ratskeller 40

(4) Townhouses 42

(5) Heterichsbrunnen 44

(6) Historiengewölbe 46

(7) Fleisch- und Tanzhaus 48

(8) St Jakob 50

◄ Dragon slayers like those at the Heterichsbrunnen
got their hands full in Rothenburg.

9 Klostergarten 54

10 Rothenburg Museum 56

11 Klingentor 58

12 St Wolfgang 60

13 Battlements 62

14 Galgentor 64

15 Röderturm 66

16 Alt-Rothenburger Handwerkerhaus 68

17 Röderbogen and Markusturm 70

18 Kapellenplatz 72

19 Weißer Turm 74

20 Judengasse 76

Burggarten, Kappenzipfel and Tauber Valley 78

21 Herrngasse 82

22 Order of Franciscans 84

23 Burgtor 86

24 Burggarten 88

25 Blasiuskapelle 90

26 Mittelalterliches Kriminalmuseum 92

27 St Johannis 94

28 Plönlein & Kobolzeller Tor 96

29 Siebersturm 98

30 Kappenzipfel 100

(31) Neues Spital 102

(32) Rossmühle 104

(33) Reichsstadthalle 106

(34) Spitaltor 108

(35) Evangelische Tagungsstätte 110

(36) Tauber Valley 112

(37) Doppelbrücke 114

(38) Kobolzeller Kapelle 116

(39) Topplerschlösschen 118

(40) St Peter und Paul in Detwang 120

(41) Rothenburg-View 122

Structure of the Guide Book

Map

Discover the hidden gems around you with the mini-map! Get inspired to take a walk and uncover exciting destinations waiting to be explored.

Number & Header

The numbers hint at an exciting tour waiting to be taken, but it is not mandatory. It is only one possible path among many. Ultimately, the choice is yours to make.

Facts and Figures

A brief introduction presents essential information about the travel point, including its fascinating history, stunning architecture, or the restructuring it may have undergone. With this well-crafted introduction, you can better appreciate your sights and make the most of your travel experience.

While facts and figures provide valuable information, they cannot replace the emotional impact of experiencing the sights firsthand.

① Marktplatz

Daten & Fakten

Am Marktplatz schlägt das Herz Rothenburgers; wie sollte den Rathaus im Westen, von Ratskellern umworben und von schmucken Bürgerhäusern eingerahmt, in denen einst Patrizier wohnten. Die Freifläche von 30 auf 50 Meter bestimmt das Leben der Bürger seit dem 13. Jahrhundert. Hier hielt die Stadt ihren Markt ab, hier wurden Verurteilte an den Pranger gestellt oder in Schauprozessen hingerichtet, hier unterwarf sich im Jahr 1631 während des Dreißigjährigen Krieges Rothenburg dem Heerführer der Katholischen Liga Johann T'Serclaes von Tilly. Am Marktplatz laufen die Fernstraßen nach Würzburg im Norden, nach Nürnberg und Augsburg im Süden und nach Ansbach im Osten zusammen. Im Zentrum der Stadt feiert Rothenburg heute den historischen Schäfertanz, die Reichsstadt-Festtage, den Meistertrunk, den Reitermarkt zu Weihnachten und viele andere Feste.

Rings um den **Marktplatz** erbauten die Bürger um 1172 die erste Stadtmauer, sie sollte den Ansiedlern einer Burg aus der Stauferzeit, die sich am Burggarten befand, Schutz gewähren. Die erste Ummauerung schloss ein Areal von 15 Hektar ein und zog sich in einem Halbkreis vom heutigen Rothenburg Museum über den Markusturm bis zur Franziskanerkirche. Die Herrngasse nach Westen entstand als Verbindung zwischen der Burg und der Stadt. Im Jahr 1241 bezeichnet eine staufische Steuerliste Rothenburg zum ersten Mal als *Civitas*; sie war bereits damals eine Ansiedlung mit halbautonomer Verwaltung. In der Stadt predigten schon im 13. Jahrhundert zwei Ritterorden: die Johanniter und der Deutsche Ritterorden. Dazu gesellten sich Dominikanerinnen und Franziskaner. Rothenburg war im Mittelalter gut mit seiner näheren Umgebung verbunden; das Taubertal lag aber niemals entlang einer bedeutenden Fernhandelsroute. Den Reichtum der Stadt erwirtschafteten die Bürger vor Ort. Der Wohlstand der Patrizier basierte auf der Zucht von Schafen, auf Tuche, Wein und dem Anbau von Getreide, das die Stadt in guten Jahren exportierte. Am Marktplatz verkauften die Bauern landwirtschaftliche Erzeugnisse; entlang der Herrngasse entstand ein Viehmarkt.

40

Background

Experience the richness of a travel point like never before by delving into its history and cultural background. Immerse yourself in the local community or discover the story of a remarkable individual who has left a lasting mark on the city. Alternatively, the secrets of a defining event are uncovered that have shaped the location into what it is today.

Structure of the Guide Book

Every traveller experiences a different world, and that enriches the community. Sharing one's impressions is the joy of the 3rd millennium. Let us embrace the beauty of diversity and come together to learn, grow, and inspire each other with our travel stories.

Diversity adds flavour to life and broadens our perspectives.

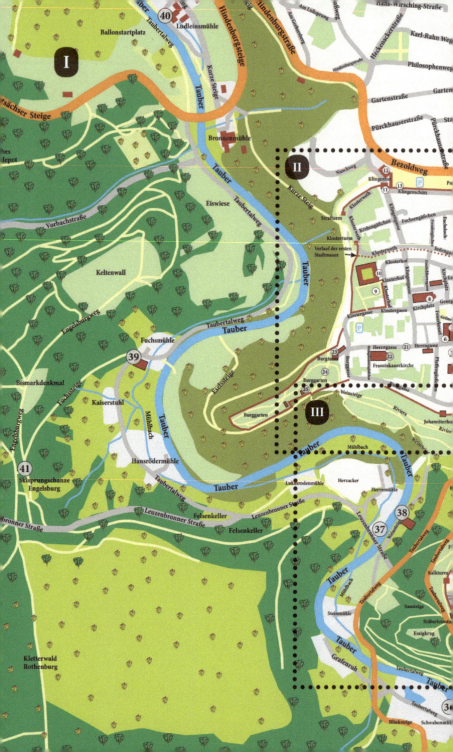

Introduction

A first Glance at Rothenburg ob der Tauber

From the Middle Ages to the 19th century, over 100 Reichststädte or Imperial Cities existed in the Holy Roman Empire. Rothenburg ob der Tauber was one of them, along with Nürnberg, Regensburg, Augsburg, Ulm, Schwäbisch Gmünd and Nördlingen. These cities were subject to the king's authority but no other power.

Like many medieval cities, Rothenburg preserved its fortifications, but hardly any other town safeguarded its historic flair as authentically. A visit to Rothenburg is a journey to the unsettling time of the Thirty Years' War. In the aftermath, the settlement fell into despair; it awoke from its deep sleep only at the turn of the century. For centuries, extreme poverty prevented the Imperial City from being rebuilt. Thus, today, the cobbled streets and medieval houses are a bewildering symbol of a long-gone culture that was fiercely independent, patriotic, federal, and above all, oligarchic.

In Rothenburg, the patricians emerged from the sodality of the Imperial Ministeriales who served the Staufer. When the dynasty fell into disgrace, the officials retained their power within the city but gained no influence beyond.

In hindsight, the demise of the Landwehr during the 17th century was no surprise: the legal form of an Imperial City, which had emerged in the High Middle Ages, could never survive - the patricians' sphere of influence was too regional. It was only a matter of time before electors, dukes or counts unified the lands to multiply their resources. Smaller towns like Rothenburg had little choice but to surrender their independence.

The history of Rothenburg is similar to that of most other Imperial Cities: As long as regional centres were the dominating force, Rothenburg maintained its autonomy. However, when a wave of consolidation started at the beginning of the modern era, Rothenburg lost its power, and the region remained gridlocked in agriculture. The burghers' mentality was medieval despite the Baroque, Rococo and Classicism emerging. It eventually embraced the Industrial Revolution and recovered when tourism searching for melancholic romanticism discovered Rothenburg at the turn of the century.

Contemporary critics argue cynically that the city is a medieval Walt Disney Park: "World War II had turned the streets into rubble; many buildings are not original, but reconstructed." The criticism hits the mark; psychologically, it makes no difference, however. Rothenburg has rebuilt the houses with a strong awareness of tradition, and the burgess preserved the city's leitmotiv with brilliant tact.

◄ **Atlantes carry the Alte Gymnasium (Old School) on their shoulders.**

A revival of interest in the Middle Ages sweeps through Germany. The country is in search of its identity and hopes by embracing the past, a different future may emerge. With its historic buildings, Rothenburg plays a vital role in integrating the lost cultures of long-gone centuries.

Along crooked alleys, half-timbered houses defy the modern age, battlements rise above the roofs, and a city wall encloses the historical centre. Picturesque? Certainly! The journey into romanticism quenches the hunger for a better world until one awakes from the fairy story and visits the Mittelalterliche Kriminalmuseum.

Rothenburg is a small town with a population of 11,000 people. However, its streets are always bustling with tourists from all over the world. Visitors from Japan, America, England and Germany come to experience the city's medieval charm. Unlike other places, Rothenburg remains unaffected by postmodernism. It provides an authentic experience of history.

The town is located above the Tauber River, where modernity meets nature. It is no wonder that Rothenburg attracts over two million visitors each year.

Rothenburg is a beautiful city at the intersection of the Burgenstraße (Castle Road) and the Romantische Straße (Romantic Road). It is 425 metres above sea level and overlooks the Tauber Valley. The stream flows 60 metres below the fortifications and adds to the magic of the city.

The hills surrounding Rothenburg are alluring, making them a perfect place to visit.

Next to agriculture, the region is renowned for tourism. Around 3000 beds and 100 restaurants, cafés and wine bars await the visitor. A wall with towers and gates surrounds the old town. Churches, monasteries, galleries and museums present the Franconian lifestyle.

The town transforms into an alluring toy museum when the locals dress up as squires or maids several times a year. At the beginning of September, Rothenburg showcases its grandeur with dancing; soldiers fire cannons, trumpets ring out, campfires are lit, and the sky is painted in flashy colours with fireworks. During Advent, the city is covered under a white robe, succumbs to cosiness, takes a bite from gingerbread, sips mulled wine and sparks Sterntaler - ice crackling under the feet.

During Pentecost, Rothenburg hosts a Franconian farce called *Der Meistertrunk* or *The Master Drink*: amateur performers reenact their version of how the city was saved after the Catholic League overtook it during the Thirty Years' War. The spectacle involves many people dressing up in medieval costumes.

The journalist Wilhelm Heinrich Riehl expressed his admiration in 1866: "A walk through the Tauber Valley is a journey through history." Wait, wait - anything changed? To this day, the church of St Jakob invites pilgrims to worship a drop of the blood of

▲ The decorations on townhouses add to the charm of the city.

Jesus. The jewel was deposited in an altar by the woodcarver Tilman Riemenschneider. The Topplerschlösschen is still reminiscent of the city's heydays. The monumental town hall still testifies the peoples' yearning for independence, and the burgher houses still radiate a sense of cosiness. And the walls? They still symbolise the unwavering determination of the citizens to defend their little sphere of influence.

Spurred on by tourism, museums have joined the canon of attractions: the Rothenburg Museum is dedicated to the city's history, while the Mittelalterliche Kriminalmuseum (Medieval Criminal Museum) focuses on the penal system. Additionally, the Alt-Rothenburger Handwerkerhaus presents the living conditions of the middle class over the ages.

Artists visited the Tauber Valley, too. They drew pencils and sketchbooks and captured the atmosphere of the landscape in their paintings. Among them were Carl Spitzweg and Ludwig Richter, pioneers of Rothenburg's tourism industry.

The sound of mills fills the air, fruit trees burst into blossom, beer gardens welcome weary visitors, and an excursion to the former Rothenburger Ski Jump offers a stunning view of the city from afar. Cyclists cross the countryside, and the Rothenburger Kletterwald offers to climb to the treetops. And let's not forget! Hearty snacks, fine wines, tasty desserts and the Schneeballen (version Rothenburg) entice the palate. Trust me! Escaping the charm of Rothenburg is impossible.

Rothenburg's History

Rothenburg's Early History

Rothenburg's history dates back to the 10th century. Life was difficult for the farmers in the Tauber Valley during that time.

The Church of St Peter und Paul in Detwang below the Burggarten (garden of the fortress) was first mentioned in 960 BC. It is the oldest chapel in the region.

Tracing Rothenburg's early history is almost impossible. Only about 400 archaeological finds exist. They comprise stone blades, axes and arrowheads, but there are too few to trace Rothenburg's early roots in detail.

From the Palaeolithic, only a single object survived. The findings from the Mesolithic are sparse, too. Traces of a long house testify the Neolithic period; burial mounds from the Hallstatt period indicate the presence of a Celtic tribe, and a settlement of Germanic people in the Landwehr documents the life of peasants under Roman rule.

Only from the time of the Merovingian dynasty (7th century) do burial tombs provide information about the lifestyle of the people in the region. The dead were buried in traditional costumes, some adorned with jewellery, some sent into the afterlife with weapons. The finds show that Rothenburg was located at the frontier between the Alemanni and the Franks.

Staufer Dynasty

In 1142, the Staufer King Konrad III constructed a fortress at today's Burggarten. By 1162, the fortress had risen to a Castrum Imperiale (Imperial Castle). Another castle, commissioned by the Grafen von Komburg, is believed to have been located at the Essigkrug near the Kappenzipfel. It was built around 1080, but no traces survived to prove its existence without doubt.

Next to the Imperial Castle, a settlement emerged at today's Rothenburg Museum towards the end of the 12th century. The farmyard provided the fortress with vital supplies, like timber, agricultural goods and labour. Until the 13th century, the parish church was in Detwang. Over the next few decades, out of the farmstead, a city emerged. In 1241, it had reached the rank of a Civita. Two knightly orders settled in Rothenburg (Order of St John and Deutscher Ritterorden). Dominicans and Franciscans followed. Gradually, the citizens constructed a defensive wall and strengthened the ring with towers, such as the Weißer Turm (White Tower) at the Georgengasse and the Markusturm (Mark's Tower) at the Röderbogen.

When the Staufer dynasty lost succession in 1250 after the death of Emperor Friedrich II, local patricians established an oligarchic regime to fill the power vacuum.

◄ The eastern and southern defensive walls are accessible and can be walked.

Imperial City

In 1274, Rothenburg became an Imperial City under King Rudolf I of Hapsburg. The magistrate pledged loyalty to the king but did not submit to any other authority. During the 13th century, Rothenburg gradually strengthened its city wall and enclosed additional quarters where craftsmen settled. The city laid the founding stone for the Church of St Jakob in 1311, which the burghers consecrated in 1485, more than 150 years later.

The so-called Rintfleisch Pogrom of 1298 killed most Jews of Rothenburg: The uprising murdered five hundred men, women and children in Rothenburg. After the outbreak of the plague in 1348/49, the Jews had to flee the Landwehr yet again. Rothenburg accused them of contaminating the wells with poison and blamed them for the outbreak of the epidemic. By 1375, the Jews had returned to the Tauber Valley and in 1407, they consecrated a synagogue at the Schrannenplatz.

It is rumoured that an earthquake caused the Imperial Castle to collapse in 1356. The citizens used the remains as a quarry and demolished the fortress. Only the Blasiuskapelle was restored. Nowadays, the chapel serves as a memorial for the victims of World War I and World War II.

After the second expansion of the city during the 14th century, the Kappenzipfel was walled in, where craftsmen and the Neue Spital (New Hospice) had settled.

During the late Middle Ages, Rothenburg had a population of around 6000 people. The city consolidated the Landwehr under Mayor Heinrich Toppler. However, attempts to participate in national politics failed: In 1407, the town went to war against Nürnberg and Würzburg but was defeated. Although the walls withstood a siege, the opponents plundered the villages and farmsteads in the Landwehr, destroying Rothenburg's livelihood. The Peace of Mergentheim was a bloodletting for Rothenburg from which the city struggled to recover. Many blamed Mayor Heinrich Toppler for the misfortune, and the magistrate incarcerated him in the dungeon of the town hall. He died there in 1408.

By 1430, Rothenburg had surrounded its almost 400 square-kilometre Landwehr with a mound known as the Landhege. The structure enclosed 167 villages and defined the territory under the city's rule.

In 1451, a rebellion headed by craftsmen attempted to gain a say in the town's administration, but the magistrate's concessions were short-lived. Soon, the city returned to its former structure and reverted to its oligarchic rule.

A devastating fire destroyed the eastern part of the town hall in 1501. Seventy years later, a new building was constructed, which brought fresh air to the Marktplatz (market square). Finally, the Renaissance had arrived at the Tauber.

▲ Rothenburg knows the way to hell - it passes through a tavern!

Reformation

When Martin Luther proclaimed his Ninety-five Theses in Wittenberg in 1517, times changed. The protest against the Church of Rome fell on fertile ground in Rothenburg. His translation of the New Testament into German became the foundation for the Peasants' Revolt four years later: "The order of society is not given by God. The Bible does not support the oppression of the peasants." A cry for freedom echoed through the streets of Rothenburg. The patricians quenched the unrest and executed their leaders at the Marktplatz.

In 1544, Rothenburg embraced the Reformation and converted to Protestantism. Consequently, the Inner Council confiscated and closed all monasteries.

Thirty Years' War

During the Thirty Years' War, Rothenburg's star plummeted. Three times opposing forces conquered the city (1631: Tilly, 1634: Piccolomini, 1645: Turenne). The Landwehr had to endure armies passing through; it had to quarter soldiers and pay for reparations. The region suffered the plague, the people starved, and the lands impoverished.

As early as 1631, the Catholic League under Johann Graf von Tilly conquered Rothenburg. Legend has it that the city was spared only because the former mayor Georg Nusch drank 13 glasses of wine in a single gulp. The amusing story is depicted at the clock of the Ratskeller. After the Thirty Years' War, Rothenburg was burdened with debt. The city only recovered in the 19th century.

Annexation by Bavaria

After the Thirty Years' War, Rothenburg fell into a deep sleep until Bavaria annexed the region in 1802/03. Napoleon restructured the German lands and rewarded Bavaria with a royal crown. He introduced a new criminal law, reformed the school system, secularised the country, and established freedom of belief. Officials in Munich oversaw the Tauber Valley; they sold the region's silverware and paid off the debt, but Rothenburg had lost its independence. From now on, Bavaria ruled by directive.

Jews returned to the city in 1870, building a synagogue, a school and a bath on Herrngasse. Unfortunately, the peace lasted only for two generations. Then, the Nazis would drive them out again. By Kristallnacht in 1938, the last Jews had fled.

Train lines connected Rothenburg to the railway in 1873. Only by then and after more than 400 years had the city recovered from the Thirty Years' War. The unification of Germany required symbols that evoked a patriotic spirit, and Rothenburg became such a vehicle. Tourists discovered the medieval town and immersed in the romanticism of national pride. Artists like Emil Kirchner and Carl Spitzweg painted the picturesque; Rothenburg had returned to a larger stage.

In 1881, the city performed the farce *Der Meistertrunk* for the first time. Two years later, the town served as a model for the design of the German pavilion at the Chicago World's Fair.

World War II

When Germany elected the Reichstag in 1933, Rothenburg voted 83% for Adolf Hitler. The fascists were popular in the Landwehr; Franconia was a stronghold of the National Socialist German Workers' Party - the slumber of the past four centuries had done no good to the city.

By October 1938 and before the Kristallnacht, the Rothenburgers had expelled the last 17 Jews from the city. In eagerness, the Tauber Valley competed with Salzburg, who had declared their city "free of any Jew" in March of the same year.

Reality hit Rothenburg at the end of World War II: an Allied air raid destroyed a third of the old town in March 1945. The detonations devastated the parts east of the Marktplatz. The city was spared a second attack, however. An exhibition in the Röderturm shows the extent of the destruction. The American John McCloy, who was later appointed High Commissioner of the US occupation zone, is said to have prevented any further bombing raids. Nevertheless, the detonations destroyed around 300 residential buildings, nine towers and 750 metres of the city wall. Many feared for Rothenburg's future as a tourist attraction.

Rothenburg submitted reluctantly when the Allied troops marched into the Landwehr to free the city on April 17, 1945. Until the final day, the SS defended the town, hiding at the Wildbad halfway above the Tauber River.

▲ Embellishments at the facade of the town hall enrich the building.

Present Day

After World War II, a significant part of the city was destroyed, and the historic atmosphere of Rothenburg was lost. Would tourism ever return? The Bayerische Denkmalamt (Bavarian Office for Monuments) took the lead and started the restoration, which was funded through donations from the public. As a token of appreciation, the city paid tribute to all patrons along the battlement. By 1960, the historic character was saved, and Rothenburg remained focused on tourism. Over time, the city expanded its offerings, converting the Zehntscheune of the Neue Spital into the Reichsstadthalle in 1975, where seminars and conferences are held today. Additionally, several Tauber festivals were introduced, and the farce *Der Meistertrunk* continued.

The Rothenburg Museum was established in the former Dominican convent in 1982. Three years later, the connection to the A7 motorway gave new impetus. A memorial stone to the city's pogroms was erected in 1998, and in 2006, Rothenburg celebrated the 125th year of the farce *Der Meistertrunk*, which draws onlookers from all over the world.

Only about 2500 people still live in the old city centre as most residential buildings were converted into cafes, restaurants and hotels, especially around the Marktplatz. Almost 50% of the guests visiting Rothenburg are from other countries.

The COVID-19 pandemic has challenged Rothenburg's tourism industry, and many businesses were struggling to survive, but Rothenburg remains resilient.

~960   **Documents mention the village Detwang in the Tauber Valley**
The Church of St Peter und Paul dates from this period. It is the oldest chapel in the region.

1080   **The Grafen von Komburg commission a fortress at the Essigkrug**
The Grafen von Komburg build a castle above the Kobolzeller Kapelle on the Essigkrug. No remains survived.

1142   **A fortress at today's Burggarten is the seed for Rothenburg**
From 1142 onwards, King Konrad III builds a fortress at today's Burggarten. It had the status of a *Castrum Imperiale* (Imperial Castle) by 1167.

1172   **City wall and town charter**
Around 1172, the first city wall is constructed. The fortification ran from today's Rothenburg Museum to the Röderbogen and the Franziskanerkirche.

~1182   **The Order of St John arrives**
Between 1182 and 1192, Emperor Friedrich I Barbarossa hands the hospice in Reichardsroth to the Order of St John.

~1227   **The Order of St John builds a hospice in Rothenburg**

1241   **Rothenburg becomes a Civitas**

1250   **Foundation of the first town hall in Gothic style**

~1245-1286 **Rabbi Meir ben Baruch lives in Rothenburg**

1250-1500 **Second city wall**
An outer battlement is constructed. The Klingentor, Galgentor and Rödertor are added. A ward provides protection, barbicans are added.

1258   **Dominican nuns move into the castle's farmyard**
At Christmas 1265, the nuns consecrate their church.

1258   **The Deutscher Ritterorden takes over the church in Detwang**

1268/69   **A city seal is mentioned, a coat of arms is known**

~1270   **Holy Blood Relic in crystallized quartz**
A drop from the cup of the Lord's Supper was transformed into the blood of Christ.

1274   **Rothenburg turns into an Imperial City**
On May 15, 1274, King Rudolf I. places Rothenburg under his direct rule. The city knows no other authority.

1280   **The Deutscher Ritterorden arrives in the city**

1280	**Founding of the Neue Spital at the Gebsattel**
	Wealthy citizens and donors from Würzburg initiate a hospice for the poor, elderly and sick at the Kappenzipfel.

1281   **The Franciscans arrive in Rothenburg**

1298   **The Rintfleisch Pogrom kills all Jews in Rothenburg**
Nearly 500 Jews are killed during the massacre.

1298   **King Albrecht I authorises the second city expansion**

1311-1484   **Construction of the Church of St Jakob**
Over 150 years, Rothenburg builds St Jakob. A Holy Blood Chapel, first mentioned in 1278, was its predecessor.

1348/49   **The Jews are driven out of the city after the plague**

1356   **An earthquake demolishes the fortress of the Staufer dynasty**

1368   **Rothenburg buys from Emperor Karl IV the right for a blood court**
Rothenburg can now intervene against critics in its ranks who potentially would endanger civil peace.

1375   **For the second time a Jewish community emerges (Judengasse)**

1376   **The Kappenzipfel is enclosed by a city wall**

1388   **Heinrich Toppler constructs the Topplerschlösschen**

1396   **The Johanniter-Komturei is built** (today Mittelalterliches Kriminalmuseum)

1397   **King Wenzel authorises the deconstruction of the fortress**

~1400   **Mayor Heinrich Toppler leads Rothenburg to a golden decade**
Rothenburg gains influence in the region; the Landwehr is strengthened.

1407   **The war against Würzburg and Nürnberg is lost**

1408   **Heinrich Toppler dies in the dungeons of the town hall**

1409   **The district court of the Landwehr is under the authority of Rothenburg**
The town has purchased the right for the district court.

1430   **The Landhege surrounding the Landwehr is built**
The city constructs a mound with towers encircling the Landwehr. The demarcation line serves to police the area.

1451-1455 **Upraising of the craftsmen**
The Äußere Rat (Outer Council) gains more say, but the political success is only short-lived. Quickly, the patricians seize power again, and the city returns to be governed by an oligarchic regime.

1466 **Friedrich Herlin carves the Zwölf-Boten-Altar in St Jakob**

1475/77 **St Wolfgang and the Brotherhood of the Shepherds are founded**

1494 **The Rothenburger Passion is painted for the Franciscans**
The 12-panel paintings are exhibited in the Rothenburg Museum.

1500-1505 **Tilman Riemenschneider carves the Heilig-Blut-Altar in St Jakob**

1516 **The Rossmühle at the Kappenzipfel is built**

1520 **Final expulsion of the Jews from Rothenburg**

1525 **The Peasants' Revolt ravages through the Landwehr**
The leaders of the Peasants' Revolt are executed at the Marktplatz.

1544 **Rothenburg joins the Reformation**
All cloisters are dissolved, services are to be held following the liturgy of the Evangelical Church.

1546/47 **Rothenburg suffers during the Schmalkaldian War**

1571 **New construction of the town hall in the style of the Renaissance**

1618 **Outbreak of the Thirty Years' War**
Rothenburg supplies troops and provides winter quarters for soldiers. Looting hordes roam the lands. Hunger and epidemics decimate the population.

1631 **Johann Graf von Tilly besieges Rothenburg**
Troops of the Catholic League besiege Rothenburg under Johann Graf von Tilly. He takes the town. The occupation serves as the backdrop to the farce *Der Meistertrunk*.

1634 **General Octavio Piccolomini besieges Rothenburg**
Piccolomini conquers Rothenburg after the Battle of Nördlingen.

1645 **General Graf Henri de Turenne besieges Rothenburg**
French soldiers take the city. Quickly, they move on.

1648 **End of the Thirty Years' War**
Rothenburg is in debt; the city has to raise 50000 guilders and falls into insignificance.

1648 Matthäus Merian the Elder engraves the view of Rothenburg

1803 **Annexation of Rothenburg by Bavaria**
With the Reichsdeputationshauptschluss, Rothenburg and parts of the Landwehr fall to Bavaria. Munich governs the city with dispatches.

1858 **Carl Spitzweg visits Rothenburg and draws a sketchbook**
The age of romanticism discovers Rothenburg. Tourism is about to become the city's primary source of income.

1864 **The Burggarten turns into a local recreation area**

1870 **The Jews return to Rothenburg**

1873 **Rothenburg is connected to the railway by a branch line**

1878 **Founding of the Arbeitsgemeinschaft für jüdische Geschichte**

1881 **Premiere of the farce Der Meistertrunk**
Rothenburg relies on tourism as an industry.

1902 **Friedrich Hessing founds the Wildbad**

1933 **Rothenburg votes 83 % for Adolf Hitler**
At the Reichstagwahlen on March 5, 1933, a total of 9,837 out of 11,851 citizens cast their votes for the Nazis.

1933-1938 **Rothenburg expels all Jews**
On October 22, 1938 (a month before Kristallnacht), the Rothenburger expel the remaining 17 Jews from the city.

1936 **The Rothenburg Museum opens in the convent of the Dominicans**

1945 **Allied air raid on Rothenburg**
On March 31, 1945, a bomb attack destroys a third of Rothenburg's old town. Parts of the medieval fortifications and some towers are destroyed. They are rebuilt after the war.

1945 **Allied troops occupy Rothenburg**
On April 17, 1945, US troops march into Rothenburg. The Wehrmacht blows up the Doppelbrücke.

1985 **A connection to the A7 motorway supports tourism**

1986 **Jorge Mario Bergoglio studies German in Rothenburg**
The future Pope Francis studies German at the Goethe-Institut in Rothenburg. The institute is closed in 2005 for reasons of profitability.

★ **Hiking in Groups:** From spring to autumn, guided tours introduce hikers to the surrounding area of Rothenburg. Thirteen hiking trails explore the natural beauty of the Landwehr around the old town.
https://www.rothenburg-tourismus.de

★ **Cycle tours in the Tauber Valley:** The ADFC presents gourmet tours through the Tauber Valley. The tour *Liebliches Taubertal* is a classic - it was awarded the highest standards.
https://www.adfc-radtourismus.de/liebliches-taubertal

★ **Winemakers and vineyards:** Some winegrowers offer guided tours through their vineyards, explain their process of production and invite to taste their wines. Numerous wine bars in Rothenburg entice to linger.
https://www.liebliches-taubertal.de

★ **Kletterwald Rothenburg:** The daring may climb to the tree tops at the magical Amerikanerwäldchen. The organisers have set up 14 courses with different levels of difficulty - for families and for enthusiasts.
https://kletterwald-rothenburg.com

★ **Balloon rides Rothenburg:** The team *Happy Ballooning* offers trips above the Tauber Valley. Even a transit over the Alps is on offer. A *Baptism of the Balloon* is part of the adventure.
https://happy-ballooning.de

★ **Workshops in the Dürerhaus:** In the Dürerhaus Grafikmuseum, amateurs may familiarise themselves with the technologies of a printing workshop. Anyone interested wants to contact the museum.
http://www.grafikmuseum-rothenburg.de

★ **Playgrounds:** Children can let off steam in Rothenburg. Numerous playgrounds along the city wall offer climbing gardens and play castles. Some are framed by wild nature.
https://www.rothenburg.de/stadtplan/stadtplan-kinderspielplaetze

★ **Cultural Events Wildbad:** The evangelical conference centre organises numerous events from retreats to concerts and debates.
https://wildbad.de/veranstaltungen-im-wildbad

★ **Theatre, concerts and workshops:** Rothenburg organises a number of performances from theatre to concerts - many are hosted on the Marktplatz. The events at the Stöberleinsbühne and the Toppler Theater are very atmospheric. The city magazine RoTour presents an overview of meditation days, discussion groups and workshops in the area.
http://www.rotour.de/veranstaltungen

★ **Guided tours:** Who wants to stroll through the streets of Rothenburg with a night watchman, roll through the old town in a vintage car or experience the Middle Ages with Walburga? Rothenburg Tourism presents a list of organisers.
https://www.rothenburg-tourismus.de/planen-buchen
www.walburga-rothenburg.de und
www.faszination-rothenburg.de

★ **Backstage Rothenburg:** Artisans reveal the secret of their trade. How is a Schneeballen created? How are chocolate fingers made? *Handmade in Rothenburg* knows the answer and offers to give it a try.
https://www.rothenburg-handmade.com

★ **Thermal Baths:** Close to Rothenburg, well-maintained swimming pools and thermal baths promise fun for the whole family. The *Franken-Therme* in Bad Windsheim offers a relaxing salt lake, wellness and sauna. The *Altmühlterme* in Treuchtlingen is popular with families. The comprehensive site *Thermen Bayern* provides an overview.
https://www.thermen-bayern.de/thermen-franken.html

★ **Fränkisches Freilandmuseum:** Bad Windsheim presents the rural life of the region - a contrast to Rothenburg's medieval urban atmosphere. The museum shows how farmers lived during the Middle Ages and how they tilled the earth.
https://freilandmuseum.de

★★ **Historiengewölbe** (→ Travel Point ⑥)

The historic vault at the rear of the town hall introduces life-sized figures of the time of the Thirty Years' War. Among them is the alchemist Andreas Libavius, who works in his laboratory. Pictures and documents explain the city's readiness for defence during the Reformation. Former Mayor Heinrich Toppler died in the dungeon in 1408.

www.meistertrunk.de

★ **Fleisch- und Tanzhaus** (→ ⑦)

Contemporary artists present their latest creations at the Fleisch- und Tanzhaus. Some works can be purchased.

Rothenburger Künstlerbund e. V. on Facebook

★ **Weihnachtsmuseum** (→ ⑦)

The Käthe-Wohlfahrts-Weihnachtsland shows how Germany enjoys the festive season around Christmas.

https://www.kaethe-wohlfahrt.com

★★★ **St Jakob** (→ ⑧)

St Jakob is the main church of Rothenburg. The House of God was consecrated in 1484. The Heilig-Blut-Altar (Holy Blood Altar) by Tilman Riemenschneider keeps a Holy Blood Relic: a drop from the chalice of the last supper had turned into the blood of Christ. It was the centre of attraction for pilgrims on their way to Rome or Santiago de Compostela. The Zwölf-Boten-Altar (Twelve Messenger Altar) by Friedrich Herlin is also worth seeing.

http://rothenburg-evangelisch.de/pfarrei-st-jakob

★★ **Klostergarten** (→ ⑨)

The garden of the former Dominican monastery awaits its visitors with wildflowers, colourful meadows and sun-kissed benches. The tranquil spot is a perfect place to take a rest. Spoiled cats visit the garden from time to time. Some of them allow to be petted.

Travel Points at a Glance

★★★ Rothenburg Museum (→ ⑩)

In the former convent of the Dominican order, Rothenburg presents its cultural and historical treasures: sandstone figures, chalices, house altars, tankards and much more. The Rothenburger Passion from 1494 depicts the suffering of Christ during his last days. The highlight of the museum is the extended kitchen of the monastery. It is the oldest in Germany.

https://www.rothenburgmuseum.de

★★ St Wolfgang (→ ⑫)

The fortified Church of St Wolfgang at the Klingentor was the prayer house of the shepherds. It was built next to the city wall in 1475. Loopholes and casemates point to the military use of the facility. A museum in the gatehouse presents Rothenburg's sheep farmers.

http://www.schaefertanzrothenburg.de

★★ Wall-Walk (→ ⑬)

Almost the entire battlement of Rothenburg is accessible. Towers, gates and cannons demonstrate the city's readiness for defence at the end of the Middle Ages. Along the 1½ metre wide corridor, the city is seen from a birds-eye view.

★ Röderturm (→ ⑮)

An exhibition in the tower room of the Röderturm presents the extent of Rothenburg's destruction at the end of World War II. On March 31, 1945, a devastating Allied air raid destroyed about a third of the old town.

https://www.alt-rothenburg.de/roederturm

★★ Handwerkerhaus (→ ⑯)

The Alt-Rothenburger Handwerkerhaus (craftsmen's house) presents the life of the craftsmen at the Tauber in a building from the Middle Ages. Weavers, shoemakers, potters and soap makers had lived in the dwelling over the past centuries. The walls of the house are crooked, the floor is clay, the beds are short.

www.alt-rothenburger-handwerkerhaus.de

★★ Grafikmuseum (→ ⑲)

The artist Ingo Domdey designed the Dürerhaus Grafikmuseum. In his workshop, he presents prints from Dürer, Rembrandt, Hrdlicka, and Janssen.

www.grafikmuseum-rothenburg.de

★★ Franziskanerkirche (→ ㉒)

The Order of Franciscans settled in the late 13th century at the Herrngasse. Die unpretentious church was consecrated in 1309. Tombstones tell of the last journey of the patricians.

http://rothenburg-evangelisch.de

★★★ Burggarten (→ ㉓ - ㉕)

Until the 14th century, an Imperial Castle built by the Staufer dynasty rose in the Burggarten (garden of the castle). Only the Blasiuskapelle survived, however. Rothenburg commemorates the fallen of the world wars at this chapel. Sandstone figures in the garden refer to the four elements and the four seasons. The view of the Tauber Valley from the Burggarten is enchanting. Gentle hills and fruit trees enrich the atmosphere.

★★★ Mittelalterliche Kriminalmuseum (→ ㉖)

The unique Mittelalterliche Kriminalmuseum (Medieval Criminal Museum) in the former Johanniter commandery introduces the legal process of the Middle Ages. The curators explain the development of the criminal and the legal system over the centuries. They show instruments of torture, neck fiddles, racks and thumbscrews. The museum is only suitable for visitors with strong nerves.

https://www.kriminalmuseum.eu

★ St Johannis (→ ㉗)

The church of the Order of St John was built at the beginning of the 15th century. The contemporary altar cross by the sculptor Klaus Backmund shows Jesus sitting on the beam of the cross. He overcame death and saves all sinners.

https://st-johannis-rothenburg.de

★★ Leyk's Lotos Garten (→ ㊲)

The entrepreneur Bernd Schulz-Leyk created an enchanting garden with exotic plants, a lake and pagodas. The entrance is on Erlbacher Straße.

https://www.lotos-garten.de

★★ Topplerschlösschen (→ ㊳)

In 1388, Heinrich Toppler had a charming castle built in the Tauber Valley. Fruit trees frame it. The raised living space presents bourgeois lifestyle from the 16th to the 19th century. The castle can be visited by prior arrangement only.

http://www.heinrich-toppler.de

★★ St Peter und Paul (→ ㊵)

The chapel in Detwang is the oldest in the region. Tilman Riemenschneider carved the impressive Heilig-Kreuz-Altar (Holy Cross Altar) around 1508.

http://rothenburg-evangelisch.de

The Church of St Jakob. ▶

Franconian cuisine is full of delightful rarities. It is traditional and rejects modern haute cuisine. Like all regions dominated by agriculture, Franconian cuisine is focused on tasteful nutrition high in calories and rich in flavour. All cuts of the meat are used as ingredients in various ways.

No eatable part of the harvest is ever lost in a peasant society. Leftovers are turned into a stew the next day, bones are used for broth. Over the centuries, the art of the kitchen has culminated into recipes that pamper all senses.

★ Schneeballen

The Schnee-ballen (snow-ball) is a treat made of short-crust pastry. The dessert is baked in the oven until the colour turns golden. Franconia and parts of Austria offer the delight (see picture). It resembles a biscuit and can be kept without refrigeration for up to four weeks. Various bakeries in Rothenburg have perfected the pastry and added tempting flavours. The Schneeballen is often enjoyed with plum schnapps and powdered sugar. Variants with chocolate, nuts, vanilla or marzipan entice anyone with a sweet tooth. Creativity has no limits.

★ Lebkuchen

The heart of Franconian Lebkuchen (gingerbread) beats in Nürnberg, but cafés in Rothenburg also offer the tasty, hand-sized slices - mostly during winter when additional calories are welcomed as a fuel against the cold weather. They want to be enjoyed with coffee or mulled wine.

The dough of the delicate wafers is made from sugar and nuts. They are baked in the oven and glazed or covered with chocolate. The delicious gingerbread has been known in Franconia since the 14th century. It truly is an irresistible treat.

★ Küchle

The doughnuts are made from a solid yeast dough. They can be as big as a plate and are usually refined with powdered sugar. They get their crispy, golden-brown colour when they are fried in oil or fat.

★ Spargel (asparagus)

In Franconia, the Spargelzeit (asparagus season) begins at the end of April and lasts until the "Asparagus New Year's Eve" on June 24th. The asparagus is grown in Franconia in the Knoblauchsland (garlic region) north of Nürnberg.

⭐ Karpfen (carp)

A delicacy in Rothenburg is the carp. The Spiegelkarpfen (mirror carp) is at home in the ponds of the neighbouring Aischgrund. During the autumn, between September and November, restaurants offer fish farmed by local breeders. (One always wants to ask where the fish was raised. The closer the pond, the fresher the carp.)

Divided in two halves, the fish is baked or served blue. Some add dark beer to the cooking. Often, the dish is served with salad and vegetables. Tender potatoes are an option, too. Enjoy the delight adding horseradish, and you become a local. And yet another hint: If the carp is freshly caught, it curls up nicely on the plate when baked.

⭐ Fränkisches Schäufele

The south of Germany specialises in pork. The Schäufele is popular in Franconia (see picture). The baked pork shoulder looks like a shovel on the plate and is very tender. The meat was cut crosswise and seasoned with cumin. With much patience, the Schäufele braises in the oven for about three hours. It is served with salad, sauerkraut and potato dumplings.

⭐ Fränkische Rostbratwurst

Grilled sausages from Nürnberg are famous around the world, and restaurants in Rothenburg offer the delicacy, too. It is a workmen's dish. The recipe may vary, but is mostly based on pork. Some butchers add veal. The sausages are often refined with marjoram.

Usually, the snack is fried on a wood-fired grill or in a large pan. The delicacy is called Saurer Zipfel (sour zip), if the sausages are cooked in vinegar. In Franconia, most taverns serve the fingers with sauerkraut. Others offer them in a bun. Sweet or hot mustard flavours the dish.

⭐ Krautwickel

The hearty stuffed cabbage is made from chopped meat wrapped in white cabbage leaves. Diced bacon is usually added. The Krautwickel are fried in a pan and served with potatoes.

⭐ Hofer Schnitz

Franconia is well-known for its hearty stews. They are perfect to use up any leftovers. The Hofner Schnitz is very popular in the Franconian Forest. It is based on carrots, kohlrabi, celery and leeks. If the kitchen still offers meat, it will be added as well.

Spring

⭐ **Frühlingserwachen (Spring Awakening):** The flowers may not yet have opened their cups, still Rothenburg is welcoming spring. At Easter, the citizens decorate the streets with twigs and painted eggs - the colourful displays are perfect targets for photographers.
https://www.rothenburg-tourismus.de

⭐ **Der Meistertrunk (Master Drink):** Rothenburg presents the Meistertrunk on the Pentecost weekend. Many citizens dress up in medieval clothes to celebrate the survival of their community during the Thirty Years' War.
www.meistertrunk.de

⭐ **Schäfertanz (Dance of the Shepherds):** At Pentecost, the shepherds dance on the Marktplatz at the Heterichsbrunnen.
http://www.schaefertanzrothenburg.de

Summer

⭐ **Rothenburger Volksfest (fair):** On the last weekend in June, the meadows south of the old town are transformed into a folk festival.
https://www.rothenburg-tourismus.de

⭐ **Taubertal-Festival**: Young adults dance to rock and hip-hop music in August for three days.
https://taubertal-festival.de

⭐ **Rothenburger Weindorf**: At the end of August, winegrowers present high-quality regional wines on the Grüner Markt (Green Market) outside the town hall.
www.facebook.com/RothenburgerWeindorf

⭐ **Reichsstadt-Festtage**: The city is turned into a medieval camp on the first weekend of September. About 25 historical groups offer spectacles and shows. The Thirty Years' War is reenacted. Torchlight processions and fireworks add to the magical atmosphere.
www.meistertrunk.de // https://www.rothenburg-tourismus.de

Autumn

⭐ **Rothenburger Märchenzauber:** At the end of October, retailers organise a fairy tale treasure hunt. Fairy tales have to be guessed. https://stadtmarketing-rothenburg.de.

⭐ **Rothenburger Herbstmesse:** At the beginning of November, Rothenburg celebrates a fair on the Schrannenplatz. For two Sundays, the old town livens up. https://www.rothenburg-tourismus.de

Winter

⭐ **Reiterlesmarkt:** In the run-up to Christmas, the streets of Rothenburg are decorated festively. The Christmas market offers gingerbread, mulled wine and decorations. The Reiterle (an angel on a horse) marches through town accompanied by children. https://www.rothenburg-tourismus.de

⭐ **Winterglühen:** During the last week before Christmas, the Burggarten presents music groups. https://www.rothenburg-tourismus.de

⭐ **Romanze an Valentin:** Romantic lights in the Burggarten on Valentine's Day motivate to bend one's knee and propose. https://www.rothenburg-tourismus.de

All-the-Year-Round

⭐ **Rothenburger Hans Sachs Spiele**: Amateur actors perform regional comedies. www.hans-sachs-rothenburg.de

⭐ **Toppler Theater**: The open-air stage at the Rothenburg Museum offers theatre and music events. http://www.toppler-theater.de

⭐ **Wochenmarkt**: On Saturdays (9:00 am - noon), a market offers goods from the region on the Marktplatz. https://www.rothenburg-tourismus.de

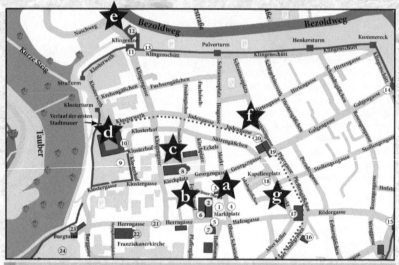

What to expect? Patrician atmosphere with medieval charm. Battlements and magnificent towers. Enticing artistic passion and romanticism.
Highlights: *Heilig-Blut-Altar* from Tilman Riemenschneider in St Jakob. The *Rothenburger Passion* in the Rothenburg Museum. The battlements at the *Klingentor*.
Duration: Approximately 4-6 hours **Entrance:** Adults 12 €

The starting point of the tour *Old Town* is at the Marktplatz in the centre of Rothenburg.

⭐ Marktplatz (→ ① - ⑤)

The market square and the surrounding buildings testify that Rothenburg was an Imperial City ruled by patricians. The Imperial Eagle at the town hall is the symbol of any free city. The town was only subordinate to the king and to no other authority. The clock at the Ratskeller performs the farce *Der Meistertrunk* every hour, and at the Heterichsbrunnen, Saint George slays yet another dragon.

⭐ Historiengewölbe (→ ⑥)

The Historiengewölbe (historic vaults) present life-sized figures of the time of the Thirty Years' War. With exhibits from the time, the museum unravels the social structure of Rothenburg during the 17th century. The curators explain the city's preparedness for defence when the Catholic League besieged the town and why Rothenburg played no further role in history after its fall. The basement of the building was once used as a dungeon. Here, the former Mayor Heinrich Toppler was starved to death.

☆ St Jakob (→ ⑧)

The Gothic church of Rothenburg is the pride of the town: it once attracted pilgrims on their way to Rome. In the west choir, a Heilig-Blut-Reliquie (a Holy Blood Relic) is guarded by an impressive altar. Tilman Riemenschneider carved the expressive figures between 1501 and 1505. They are a milestone in art history at the brink of the Middle Ages to modernity. Instead of archetypal images, the artist shows the characters with human traits and emotions. Worth seeing are the Zwölf-Boten-Altar (Twelve Messengers) by Friedrich Herlin and the Maria-Krönungs-Altar (Coronation of Mary).

☆ Rothenburg Museum (→ ⑨ ⑩)

On the way to the Rothenburg Museum, housed in the former Dominican convent, one passes the Klostergarten (former garden of the convent), which once was used as an herb garden and today inspires to meditate.

The Rothenburg Museum shows the history of the city from its beginnings to the present day. The moving Rothenburger Passion (Rothenburg Passion), which was created around 1494 for the Franciscan monastery, impresses with its rough portrayal of the characters. The kitchen of the monastery is the oldest surviving in Germany. The 19th century picturesque paintings of the city are admirable.

☆ Wall-walk (→ ⑪ - ⑬)

The first city wall ended at the street Klosterweth. The Klingentor (Blade Gate) is part of the city expansion and was added around 1400. A stairway leads to the battlement. One wants to take a walk along the wall. The path is almost four kilometres long. To circumnavigate the town takes about 2 ½ hours.

The fortified Church of St Wolfgang is adjacent to the Klingentor. It was the shepherd's house of worship. A museum introduces the Brotherhood of Shepherds. The fortifications of the church are best studied from the road Bezoldweg. Casemates cover the ground. They served as a means to defend the city.

☆ Weißer Turm (→ ⑲ ⑳)

The Weißer Turm (White Tower) was a part of the first city fortification, completed at the end of the 12th century. From 1375 onwards, Rothenburg's second Jewish settlement was situated along the Judengasse. The Dürerhaus Grafikmuseum introduces the art of printing.

☆ Röderbogen (→ ⑰)

The Röderbogen was a part of the first city wall. Storks frequently nest on its roof.

A detour to the Alt-Rothenburger Handwerkerhaus (a traditional craftsmen's house) introduces the life of Rothenburg's craftsmen from the Middle Ages to the present times.

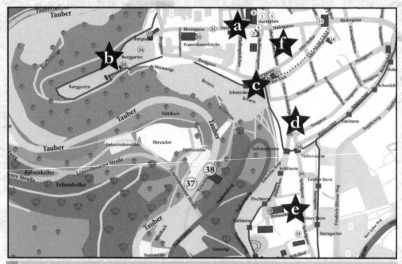

What to expect? Lovely gardens and enchanting nature. Birds eye view of the Tauber Valley, fruit trees, medieval hospices and torture. Scenic shopping.
Highlights: At the *Burggarten*, Rothenburg set its foot into history. The *Mittelalterliche Kriminalmuseum* shocks. The *Plönlein* is Germany's most romantic spot.
Duration: Approximately 4-6 hours **Entrance:** Adults 8 €

The tour starts at the Herrngasse close to the Marktplatz.

★ Herrngasse (→ ㉑ ㉒)

In the Middle Ages, the Herrngasse connected the Staufer castle with the town hall at the Marktplatz. Patricians settled close to the fountain depicting a water woman. The design of the houses provide an idea of the lifestyle of the upper class. Nowadays, several inns and restaurants serve authentic local cuisine. The Franciscans established their order on Herrngasse during the 13th century.

★ Burggarten (→ ㉓ - ㉕)

In the 12th century, the Staufer dynasty built a castle, of which only the Blasiuskapelle survived. Legend has it that the fortress collapsed during an earthquake in 1356. Subsequently, it was demolished. The chapel hosts a memorial dedicated to those who lost their lives during the world wars.

The romantic garden of the former castle is a good spot to take a stroll. From the surrounding wall, the eye catches a glimpse of the Tauber Valley. Sandstone figures depict the four seasons and the four elements.

☆ Kriminalmuseum (→ 26, 27)

The *Mittelalterliche Kriminal-museum* (Medieval Crime Museum) offers a touching exhibition on the legal system of southern Germany throughout the centuries. Its display is unique in Germany. The curators showcase criminal proceedings and the execution of sentences since the Middle Ages. Notorious criminals, witches and wizards are introduced. The exhibition features both honorary and capital punishments. A visit is not for the fainthearted, however.

The museum is situated in the former Johanniter Commandery built in the 14th century. The knights of the Order of St John settled in the Landwehr during the 12th century. Their temple, the Church of St Johannis, is next to the museum. It was once a popular stopover for pilgrims on their way to Rome or Santiago de Compostela.

☆ Plönlein (→ 28 29)

The Plönlein is considered to be Germany's most romantic spot. It featured in numerous films after World War II. The location served as an inspiration for the 1940 film Pinocchio. The farmers of Rothenburg once kept fresh fish for sale in a trough at the fountain. To the west, the path runs to the Tauber Valley and the Doppelbrücke. Towards the south, the Siebersturm separates the suburb Kappenzipfel from the old town.

☆ Kappenzipfel (→ 30 - 34)

A visit to the neighbourhood *Kappenzipfel* gives a glimpse of Rothenburg's former Hospice of the Holy Spirit at the Spitaltor called *Neues Spital*. It was founded during the 13th century. At that time, it was the wealthiest institution in Rothenburg; it cared for the poor, elderly and needy.

The suburb is home to the impressive Rossmühle, which once pumped drinking water from the Tauber River into the city. Today, it serves as a youth hostel. The barn opposite is a reminder of the importance of sheep breeding in the Landwehr. The Stöberleinsbühne stages open-air events. The amphitheatre is an excellent spot to take a break or have a relaxing picnic surrounded by urban nature.

☆ Obere Schmiedgasse

The tour returns via the Obere Schmiedgasse to the Marktplatz. Numerous shops offer regional products along the ascending street - including souvenirs and delicious chocolate. A medieval shop sells clothes in the style of Rothenburg's Middle Ages.

Alternatively, one may take a short detour along the Röderschütt to the impressive Röderturm. In the Turmstube (tower room), the Verein Alt-Rothenburg (Alt-Rothenburg Association) presents an exhibition that shows the city's destruction after World War II.

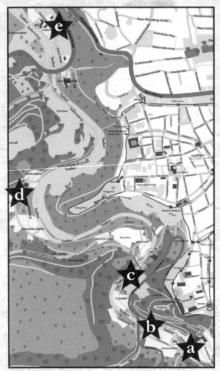

☆ Wildbad (→ 35)

During the 14th century, shepherds stumbled upon a sulphur spring on the slope just below Rothenburg. Later, in the 19th century, an upscale spa hotel opened, which became a popular destination for city dwellers seeking relaxation and medical care. Since 1978, the former Wildbad houses an Evangelical Conference Centre, which offers retreats and cultural events. Visitors may admire the serene gardens surrounding the complex.

☆ Tauber Valley & Mills (→ 36)

Rothenburg's busy mills once turned along the Tauber Valley, generating the city's wealth rotation by rotation. Some of these buildings can still be identified today. In the late 19th century, the Wildbad spa hotel utilised the Schwabenmühle to cultivate fruits and vegetables for their guests.

The Tauber River rushes wildly along the slope, surrounded by dense forests and lush meadows. Fishing once supported the people's nutrition, and big game roamed the woods. Foxes, rabbits and badgers can still be spotted in the area, while dippers and kingfishers may appear on the river banks on quiet days.

The Tauber Valley tour starts from the parking lot near the Evangelical Conference Centre. Alternatively, one may descend from the Spitaltor along a winding path (Hessingstrasse) to the Tauber River. One wants to be cautious as the path is steep and can be slippery.

What to expect? Wild nature, a rushing river, lush meadows, orchards and the silhouette of Rothenburg. Civic grandeur, popular piety and romanticism.
Highlights: The *Topplerschlösschen* was built by Heinrich Toppler around 1388. The church of *St Peter und Paul in Detwang* is the oldest in the region. Its altar is by Tilman Riemenschneider.
Duration: Around 6-8 hours **Entrance:** Adults 2€

✪ Doppelbrücke (→ ㊲)

The *Doppelbrücke*, a bridge built in the 14th century, facilitated the long-distance trade between Frankfurt and Nürnberg. The steep climb over the Kobolzeller Steige to Rothenburg was challenging and required additional horses, an extra income for the burghers of Rothenburg.

In 1945, during the Nazi retreat, the Wehrmacht destroyed the bridge to hinder the advancement of the Allied troops. Rothenburg rebuilt the crossing later.

The path along the Weinsteige leads to the Kobolzeller Kapelle, which citizens destroyed during the Reformation.

Detour: Via the Leuzenbronner Straße, one arrives at the hill of the former Rothenburger ski jump, from where Matthäus Merian the Elder engraved the view of Rothenburg. South of the Engelsburg, the Rothenburger Kletterwald awaits the brave-hearted who dare to be challenged by the adventurous courses.

✪ Topplerschlösschen (→ ㊴)

Around 1388, the former mayor Heinrich Toppler commissioned the homely Topplerschlösschen below the Burggarten. An orchard surrounds it. The private property can only be visited by appointment.

Heinrich Toppler was an ambitious mayor of Rothenburg in the 14th century who strengthened the city's influence over the Landwehr. When Würzburg challenged Rothenburg's right to be governed as an Imperial City, Toppler defended the oligarchic regime. However, Rothenburg lost the ensuing war, and Heinrich Toppler lost his life in the dungeon of the town hall in 1408.

On the eastern bank of the wild Tauber River, and shortly after the Topplerschlösschen, one encounters the Bronnenmühl, a delightful beer garden and once a mill which pumped water to the Klingentor. Last but not least, the Taubertal Festival takes place every year at the nearby Eiswiese.

✪ Detwang (→ ㊵)

The Church of St Peter und Paul in Detwang is the oldest place of worship in the region. It was first mentioned around 960. The village was established before Rothenburg, and during the early days of the city, the parish was responsible for Rothenburg until St Jakob took over the services. The two churches are closely intertwined.

Tilman Riemenschneider crafted the impressive Heilig-Kreuz-Altar around 1513. It has been in the church since 1653. Previously, it was used to give the last escort to the citizens at the Michaelskapelle. The prayer house was Rothenburg's funeral chapel, located opposite St Jakob. Today, it is a restaurant with a beer garden. The building was demolished when the cemetery was relocated.

The best way to return to Rothenburg is via the Kurze Steige; it branches off at the Bronnenmühle.

Walkabouts

The Magic of Rothenburg

Rothenburg is a small town in Franconia, Bavaria. Until the turn of the century, about 6,000 people lived within the medieval enclosure. Today, only around 2,500 still maintain the traditions of bygone days. About 10,000 citizens reside in the new development areas outside the old town. They were built to the north and east of Rothenburg after World War II. *"Excuse me: how do I get to the torture chamber, please?"* - *"Follow that path. It is just around the corner."* - *"Thank you, very kind indeed."* - *"My pleasure."*

Each day, around 5,000 to 10,000 tourists visit the fortified walls. Along the principal axes, they are in the majority during the day: families with children, lovers holding hands, witches with dogs, globetrotters on the way from there to nowhere, members of a sports club, young ladies who sweeten a friend's evening before the wedding, Japanese with souvenirs under their arms, Americans with wide-brimmed hats and cameras around their necks. *"May I ask you something? The master drink! Does the clock show it every hour?"* - *"Yes."* - *"Aha! Does it take long?"* - *"No. We drink fast."*

Rothenburg lives for a day, swaps tourists the next morning and is confronted with the same questions. The scene repeats itself hour by hour. Over and over again. Only the weather changes - and the season - sometimes. The faces are different though - or are they ... really? *"Sorry - are you from Rothenburg? I'm looking for the museum!"* - *"Which one?"* - *"Oh, there are several?"*

Teenagers stroll across the market square, holding cigarettes. Girls smear ice cream on their noses; boys rush along the battlement, wooden swords drawn to the sky. Older gentlemen sip coffee; ladies show off their skin to the sun; a long-beard opens a can and leans casually against his motorcycle. Pilgrims seek the blood of the Saviour, cleansing their souls with glory. *"Excuse me: Can one view this house?"* - *"Private!"* - *"Oh, I didn't know. What a pity! Could I still ... nevertheless?"*

Market square, town hall, dungeon, St Jakob, fortified church, city wall, a view over the Tauber Valley, a second view over the Tauber Valley, a detour to the old New Hospital: *"I'm looking for my car. Do you know where I parked it?"* - *"No!"* - *"Oh, how outrageous!"*

Anyone living in Rothenburg needs nerves made of steel.

◄ **A knight stands guard at the town hall to protect the citizens.**

Rothenburg's Old Town

Insiders know ...

Rothenburg from a Birds-Eye View

Tower guards once protected the city at the town hall. The viewing platform offers a breathtaking scene of the old town and the Tauber Valley. The battlements and the Röderturm also allow a birds-eye view.

Junker or Maid - beware

Who wants to experience the Middle Ages as a Junker or Maid? You want to dress up during the Reichsstadt-Festtage in September or during the Historische Festspiele at Pentecost when campfires crackle fiercely.

On the Trail of the Shepherds

Rothenburg once was a stronghold of the shepherds. Not only does the shepherd's dance remind us. There is a shepherd's museum at the Church of St Wolfgang, and one of their barns still survived in the Kappenzipfel.

The Mother of all Kitchens

The Rothenburg Museum offers many attractions from the city's history. It presents the oldest kitchen in Germany, and the Rothenburger Passion shows the story of Jesus's suffering.

Christmas - all Season-'round

The Weihnachtsmuseum (Christmas Museum) on Herrngasse is open all year round: Saint Nicholas, angels and nutcrackers want to be admired. Or wait until Advent and sip mulled wine with Christ the child!

The Artists' best Works

Tilman Riemenschneider carved the Heilig-Blut-Altar for the Pilgrim Church of St Jakob. His vibrant art gets under anyone's skin. Another of his works can be found in Detwang. You have to admire it!

Pay Attention to the Fountains

Rothenburg is poor in drinking water so mills pumped water from the Tauber River to the city. The city's wells were not reaching the groundwater; they were cisterns that collected rainwater.

The Storks of Rothenburg

In Rothenburg, storks glide over the roofs of the city. Their flight is graceful, and they nest at the Markusturm. Why? To secure the offspring of Rothenburg - of course!

◄ The town hall of Rothenburg dominates the Marktplatz.

1. Marktplatz 36
2. Town Hall 38
3. Ratskeller 40
4. Townhouses 42
5. Heterichsbrunnen 44
6. Historiengewölbe 46
7. Fleisch- und Tanzhaus 48
8. St Jakob 50
9. Klostergarten 54
10. Rothenburg Museum 56
11. Klingentor 58
12. St Wolfgang 60
13. Battlements 62
14. Galgentor 64
15. Röderturm 66
16. Rothenburger Handwerkerhaus . . 68
17. Röderbogen & Markusturm 70
18. Kapellenplatz 72
19. Weißer Turm 74
20. Judengasse 76

The Heterichsbrunnen at the Marktplatz
babbles and babbles and babbles. ▶

Rothenburg's heart beats at the *Marktplatz*. The fate of the city was decided by the patricians at the *town hall*; at the *Ratskeller,* they celebrated their festivals. In the centre of the settlement, the influential members of the Inner Council resided in spacious townhouses, and the *Heterichsbrunnen* was the source of water for the citizens.

Twice a year, the magistrate organises medieval spectacles in the old town. They turn the streets into an open-air festival. During these events, people dress up in costumes and wave flags, heavy drums fill the air, cannons fire, and amateur actors put on the farce *Der Meistertrunk* wearing brightly-coloured robes.

The *Historiengewölbe* presents defining scenes from the region's history. At the *Fleisch- und Tanzhaus*, local artists present contemporary art available for purchase. The Church of *St Jakob* is the pride of the settlement and an expression of self-confident independence that refused to submit to anyone but the king. Tilman Riemenschneider's Heilig-Blut-Altar bears witness to the piety of the people to this very day.

The enchanted *Klostergarten* was once part of the Dominican monastery. Next door, the *Rothenburg Museum* introduces the history of the city. The museum's highlight is the Rothenburger Passion, which tells the story of Jesus's suffering.

The *Klingentor* is the perfect place to experience the charm of the city fortifications. The Church of *St Wolfgang* is a testament to the citizens' willingness to defend their settlement in the Middle Ages. The church was once used by shepherds for worship.

The battlement can be explored from the *Klingentor* to the *Kappenzipfel,* testifying how Rothenburg protected its burghers from attacks during the Middle Ages. Nevertheless, the city was captured several times during the Thirty Years' War. The *Galgenturm* was also a part of the second city wall. The tower room at the *Röderturm* displays pictures and documents illustrating the extent of destruction in Rothenburg after World War II.

From the Middle Ages to the present times, craftsmen, earning their living in different trades, worked and lived at the *Alt-Rothenburger Handwerkerhaus*. The museum shows their everyday life without running water or electricity.

The *Röderbogen*, the *Markusturm* and the *Weißer Turm* are among the oldest buildings in the city. They were part of the first city wall. Today, the *Dürerhaus Grafikmuseum* showcases intaglio prints from five centuries. In the Middle Ages, Jews lived on *Kapellenplatz* and *Judengasse*. They worked, raised their families and celebrated their faith in this neighbourhood.

① Marktplatz

Facts & Figures

The beating heart of Rothenburg pounds at the Marktplatz. The square is framed by the town hall in the west, the Ratskeller in the north and spacious townhouses in the east and south. There, patricians once resided. This open space of 30 by 50 metres has defined the lives of the citizens since

the 13th century. Here, the city held its market; here, convicts were pilloried or executed in show trials, and here, in 1631, during the Thirty Years' War, Rothenburg surrendered to the military leader of the Catholic League, Johann Graf von Tilly. The market square is where the main roads to Würzburg in the north, Nürnberg and Augsburg in the south, and Ansbach in the east intersect. Rothenburg celebrates many festivals in the city centre, such as the historic Schäfertanz (Shepherd's Dance), the Reichsstadt-Festtage (Imperial City Festival), the farce *Der Meistertrunk*, and the Reiterlesmarkt at Christmas.

The burgess constructed the first city wall around the **Marktplatz** in 1172. The wall was built to protect the servants of an Imperial Castle, which was erected by the Staufer dynasty at today's Burggarten. The first wall enclosed an area of 13 hectares and stretched in a circle from today's Rothenburg Museum via the Markusturm to the Franciscan Church. The Herrngasse to the west was layed out to connect the castle to the city. In 1241, a tax document mentioned Rothenburg as a Civitas. At that time, it was a settlement with semi-autonomous administration. During the 13th century, two knightly orders, the Order of St John and the Deutscher Ritterorden settled in the city. The Dominicans and the Franciscans followed soon after.

During the Middle Ages, Rothenburg was closely linked with the surrounding Landwehr. However, the Tauber Valley was never connected to any significant long-distance trading route. The city's wealth was generated locally. The patricians' prosperity was based on sheep breeding, cloth manufacturing, wine production and grain, which the community exported in good years. Nearby farmers offered their agricultural products at the market square. Livestock was traded along the Herrngasse.

▲ The Marktplatz is the beating heart of Rothenburg. Here, the city celebrates its festivals.

Rothenburg is a tranquil city that never gained national significance. After the Thirty Years' War, history forgot the town.

As an Imperial City, Rothenburg had jurisdiction over its citizens. The pillory was located at the town hall (corner of Herrngasse). In 1525, the city staged a show trial outside the Ratskeller and executed many leaders of the Peasants' Revolt.

At the corner of Hafengasse, a militant bagpiper plays a strange tune. The statue was designed by the Rothenburg sculptor Johannes Oertel, who enjoyed his artistic heydays during the Nazi regime while being an active member of Adolf Hitler's NSDAP.

Location: Marktplatz **Entrance:** Without charge **Opening times:** Always accessible
Internet: https://www.rothenburg-tourismus.de
City Magazine: http://www.rotour.de

The Bagpiper from Rothenburg

During the Thirty Years' War, the plague raged through Rothenburg. One day, the pantaloon Augustin stumbled out of a tavern at night - he was drunk - fell over his bagpipe and passed out. At midnight, the gravediggers collected his corpse, loaded him onto their cart and took him to a mass grave at the Jewish cemetery. The following day, Augustin woke up trapped between rotting bones. In despair, he screamed for help, but nobody noticed him - his shouting was in vain. Finally, the gravediggers heard the faint sound of a bagpipe - and they were scared - terribly scared: "The deaths are rising; Judgment Day is upon us!" After a while, the frightened Rothenburgers summoned all their courage, opened the grave and found the drunkard. One more time, Augustin had escaped the devil's clutches.

Town Hall

Facts & Figures

After the town hall had fallen victim to a fire in 1240, the burghers reconstructed the building in Gothic style ten years later. In 1501, yet another fire turned the eastern part into rubble. From 1572 onward, Leonhard Weidmann built the section facing the market square in Renaissance style. In 1681, Kaspar Flürlein added the baroque arcade, making the town hall an amalgam of three styles. Rothenburg had been an Imperial City since 1274, and the magistrate demonstrated their independence with a Reichsadler (Imperial Eagle) above the entrance: "We are only subjects of the king and have no other master." Along the arcade, they placed the coats of arms of Germany's eight electors, none of whom they needed to highlight! There are exactly 220 steps leading up to the 55-metre-tall gable tower (count children, count!). The platform offers an enchanting view of the city.

The **town hall** in Rothenburg is more than merely the location where the magistrate holds its sessions; it is a monumental symbol of the balance of power in an Imperial City that has always aimed for independence since its founding. In the city republic, an oligarchic government emerged with the rise of the patricians. Like Nürnberg or Amsterdam, the town hall bears witness to this political reality. Throughout history, the class system was marked by a strict dress code, and the style of a townhouse was indicative of one's rank in society.

At the city's administrative centre, the patricians spoke justice, decided on war and peace, organised the construction of the city wall, collected taxes and defined the services of the farmers and citizens. The Zeughaus (armoury) was located in the eastern part. At the corner of Herrngasse, the Inner Council kept the weights traders had to use at the market. The pillory stood there, too - elevated for better visibility.

Guards stood watch in the adjacent tower, looking out for thieves and fires. They imprisoned delinquents in the dungeon of the town hall. In 1408, the former mayor Heinrich Toppler was one of the prisoners. According to legend, the burghers forgot him, and he eventually died of thirst.

A spiral staircase leads to the vestibule on the first floor. The coats of arms evoke the patricians of Rothenburg. A painting by Ernst Unbehaben shows Heinrich Toppler. The impressive Gothic Imperial Hall is now used for events, weddings and the annual performance of the farce *Der Meistertrunk*.

In the Middle Ages, sales stands were erected in the town hall's atrium between the building's two parts. They can still be traced. Close by, the Historiengewölbe displays the city's history. The steps facing the arcades to the Marktplatz offer a perfect place to rest, ponder, meditate and exchange the latest news - just like in olden times.

▲ The town hall of Rothenburg is a symbol of the power of the patricians.

Location: Marktplatz **Town Hall:** Mo - Fr 8.00 - 12.00 **Tower:** Entrance 2,50 €
Opening Times: 9.30 - 12.30 / 13.00 - 17.00, Winter 12.00 - 15.00
Advent 10.30 - 14.00 / 14.30 - 18.00 **Internet:** https://www.rothenburg.de

Mayor Georg Nusch

Georg Nusch was a trained solicitor who famously outwitted Johann Graf von Tilly, the leader of the Catholic League. For 400 years, he has been considered the very hero of Rothenburg and a symbol of the Franconians' fight for freedom. Nusch was born on January 8, 1588, as the son of a patrician at the tavern Roter Hahn. Wine was his mother's milk: Bronnbacher, Volkacher and later, as a Latin student at the Franciscan monastery, he dedicated himself to Malvasia. While working as an assistant to a notary, he enjoyed the wines of the Rhineland. During his studies in Tübingen, he delved into their vines, and on his trips to France and Italy, he got to know the winemakers of the south, with a particular fondness for the Tuscan wines. Nush was well prepared for the challenge when he crossed paths with his opponent, Johann Graf von Tilly, in 1631.

③ Ratskeller

Facts & Figures

The patricians used to get together at the Ratskeller after their meetings at the town hall to enjoy wine. Similar to London's prestigious clubs, only the established families had access to the tavern, and many decisions were made during the merry banquets and not in the town hall.

The burghers constructed the elegant building with a baroque facade and a slender roof in 1446. The city scales were once kept on the ground floor, where the Rothenburg Tourism Service welcomes visitors today. Next to it was the primary guard station. Since 1910, Rothenburg has commemorated the farce *Der Meistertrunk* at the clock; the story is played on the hour. Former mayor Georg Nusch (right) empties 13 glasses of wine in one go while facing Johann Graf von Tilly on the other side. The city clock under the Imperial Eagle was added in 1683; the sundial above dates from 1768.

Every year at Pentecost, Rothenburg hosts a festival that historians classify as a legend: **Der Meistertrunk**. Junkers and maids in historical costumes enthusiastically march into the city, singing, dancing and spreading joy. Timpani, trumpets and flutes accompany the festive procession. In the Imperial Hall of the Rathaus, amateurs perform a play that depicts how the Protestant city was saved from the overwhelming army of the Catholic League during the Thirty Years' War.

Johann Graf von Tilly conquered Rothenburg on October 30, 1631, leaving the city for his soldiers open to take; all patricians were to be executed. The citizens feared a fate similar to that of Magdeburg: the Catholic League had razed the city to the ground half a year before. The massacre went down as the *Sack of Magdeburg*. When Johann Graf von Tilly was offered a tankard containing 3¼ litres of wine, he suggested a bet: "*If one of you has the strength and courage to empty the cup in one go, I will spare the city.*"

Former mayor Georg Nusch stepped forward, smiled and emptied the tankard in ten minutes. He then slept for three days. Johann Graf von Tilly kept his promise and showed mercy. The city was saved, and

▲ The clock shows the legend of the Meistertrunk on the hour.

the people rejoiced. The Rothenburg Museum proudly displays the tankard to prove the outrageous legend. The story, therefore, must be true!

The farce originated in the 18th century. Adam Hörber, a Rothenburg master glazier and poet, rewrote the story and transformed it into a drama premiered in 1881.

Finally, the day has arrived: Everyone in Rothenburg is ready for the festivities, and the townhouses serve as a backdrop. Young men in medieval uniforms march through the city with historical weapons - cannons fire at the camp next to the Galgentor. Horse-drawn carts rattle over the pavement, and the maids keep themselves entertained at the campfire.

Rothenburg Tourism Service: Marktplatz 2 **Telephone** 09861 404-800
Opening Times: Mon – Fri 9.00 – 17.00, Weekends from 10.00 onwards
Internet: https://www.rothenburg-tourismus.de // www.meistertrunk.de

The Reichsstadt-Festtage

The Middle Ages are thriving in Germany. Not only do the citizens dress in traditional costumes during the Landshut Wedding, but also Rothenburg plunges into the past. On the first weekend in September, people wear colourful clothes and turn the city into an open-air stage. Knights and junkers, noble ladies and patricians, torchlight and marching bands, campfires and dances delight thousands of people travelling from nearby and far. Fireworks at the town hall conclude the first day; "*The Burning City*" illuminates the night of the second day. More than 25 groups present historical episodes from the life of the people in the Landwehr: skeletons swing scythes, monks show lustful empathy, shepherds perform a jolly dance, witches sell love poisons, and old ladies tell gruesome Fairy Tales.

Townhouses

Facts & Figures

Many patricians of Rothenburg built their houses around the Marktplatz, being conscious of their social rank. The wealth of the city was generated locally; only a few were involved in long-distance trade. The influential families showed no ambitions nationally or internationally. Historians speculate that Rothenburg's first town hall may have been at today's Marien-Apotheke. The Jagstheimer family, who had a mayor as their member, lived in the adjacent Jagstheimerhaus from 1488 onwards. The Virgin Mary blesses the burghers at the bay window. In 1513, Emperor Maximilian I spent the night there. The house on Obere Schmiedgasse 5 commemorates the Toppler family. Heinrich Toppler was a mayor of the city in the 14th century, and he constructed the building at this time. Today, the Gasthof zum Greifen offers traditional cuisine in his former residence.

During the 14th and 15th centuries, around 6,000 burghers resided inside the walls of Rothenburg. Those who received citizenship enjoyed privileges but were obliged to support the community. If necessary, they had to sacrifice their lives. Only those with citizenship could settle in Rothenburg, practice a craft, and avoid outside courts. In return, they had to defend Rothenburg, keep the city wall in good condition, and pay taxes to the council; they had to patrol the streets, and the magistrate organised them into vigilantes.

The daily life of the burghers in an Imperial City differed only little from that in any other city. The mayor and the Inner Council were recruited from a small group of patrician families. They were responsible for making all essential decisions that affected the future of the Landwehr; they controlled every aspect of life within the walls. The citizens' political influence on the community's fate was advisory.

During the Middle Ages, the mortality in cities exceeded the birth rate; as with any other city, Rothenburg depended on immigration, too. The cramped living conditions often led to epidemics and hunger; war always swung its scythe over the heads of the people.

▲ The Baumeisterhaus was constructed in the style of the Renaissance in 1596.

The powerlessness of the citizens led to uprisings at times, including a demand for more rights in 1451, when the people overwhelmed the Inner Council. However, the revolt petered out only four years later.

The Rothenburgers also supported the Peasants' Revolt in 1525: *"Nothing separates citizens and farmers but a wall."* this was the saying when the people rebelled against the patricians.

As in any other city, the middle class in Rothenburg played only a minor role. The degree of self-government of the craftsmen was limited throughout history. The patricians even controlled their private life.

Location: Marktplatz, Obere Schmiedgasse, Herrngasse
Entrance: Without charge **Opening Times:** Always accessible
Internet: https://www.baumeisterhaus-rothenburg.de

The Baumeisterhaus

A refreshing building awaits the visitor at Obere Schmiedgasse 3, which breaks up the medieval atmosphere of the old town with its Renaissance facade. The townhouse was built from sandstone around 1596 for the Hirsching family. Michael Hirsching was a member of the Inner Council. As council architect, he was responsible for urban construction. The facade is adorned with a total of 14 figures, representing the seven virtues (bravery, justice, goodness of heart, motherliness, gentleness, prudence and temperance) alongside the seven vices (stinginess, unchastity, pride, falsehood, sloth, gluttony and fraud). The figures were replaced by copies in 1936, with the weathered originals preserved at the Rothenburg Museum. The building's picturesque inner courtyard is perfect for relishing some delicious home-cooked food.

⑤ Heterichsbrunnen

Facts & Figures

The Heterichsbrunnen (also called Marktplatzbrunnen or St Georgsbrunnen) is an eight-metre-deep water reservoir that can hold up to 100,000 litres of water. The Heterichsbrunnen is the largest fountain in the city, built in 1446. The Rothenburg sculptor Christoph Körner designed the dodecagonal basin in Renaissance style around 1608. Saint George overcomes a dragon with his lance at the top of the richly adorned central column, decorated with coats of arms. The citizens pumped the water to the cistern from a spring outside the city using a secret pipe, making it difficult for besiegers to find the source. Every year, the shepherds of Rothenburg danced around the fountain to drive the plague out of the Landwehr - and they still do today. On Saturday mornings, a vibrant farmers' market sells biologically grown groceries between the fountain and the Ratskeller.

Rothenburg's prosperity is driven by its thriving agriculture. Farmers cultivated the hilltops with grains; vineyards covered the slopes, fishermen angled in the Tauber River, and sheep grazed everywhere in between. The **shepherds** were such an integral part of the city's income that they formed a brotherhood. They enriched the image of the landscape. Next to meat, the animals gave wool - and the Rothenburgers processed it into fine cloth. A patrician became wealthy mainly through property ownership. He would buy impoverished estates and increase his standing by demanding tributes from the farmers.

The Church of St Wolfgang at the Klingentor was dedicated to the shepherds. Saint Wolfgang is the patron saint of the shepherds. He protects their herds from straying wolves and other dangers. Since 1517, shepherds from the Landwehr have been making a pilgrimage to Rothenburg on St Wolfgang's Day to worship the Lord, and the day always ended with dance and music. Legend has it that these celebrations drove the plague out of the city, and nine months later, many children were born. Others believe that the dance originated from a shepherd dreaming of a treasure. The tradition of the shepherd's dance is repeated every year at Pentecost

▲ The Rothenburgers erected the Heterichs-brunnen at the Marktplatzas in 1446.

during the Reichsstadt-Festtage. The city revived this tradition in 1911.

Shepherds were not welcomed in cities. Their animals caused epidemics and illnesses. That's why the Church of St Wolfgang is located on the city's outskirts, not in the centre of Rothenburg.

In 1476/77, an upbeat wool merchant named Michael Otnat founded the Brotherhood of Shepherds. The Rothenburgers had been breeding sheep on a large scale since the 14th century, and their cloth was sold as far as Italy. The brotherhood aimed to organise trade and protect individuals from misfortune by creating an early form of community insurance.

Location: Marktplatz **Entrance:** Without charge **Opening times:** Always accessible
Internet: http://www.schaefertanzrothenburg.de
Rothenburger Hans Sachs Spiele: www.hans-sachs-rothenburg.de

The Hans Sachs Spiele

For a century, actors in the tradition of the Nürnberg poet Hans Sachs have delighted their visitors with Franconian mischief. The Toppler Theater at the Rothenburg Museum is their main stage, but they also performed at other venues. Musicians accompany them with traditional songs from the region. The theatre was founded in 1921 by Theodor Schletterer; Theodor wanted to entertain the people with his stories. Initially, the group performed in taverns. The amateur actors are committed to preserving dialect poetry and take a satirical stance on Franconian's social structure. The characters are archetypal and reflect the spirit of the ordinary people: a cunning farmer who sells a scrawny cow, a priest who exorcises a citizen from a ghost, a crafty wife who stands up to her husband, young lovers who get married against the will of their parents.

6 Historiengewölbe

Facts & Figures

The Historiengewölbe at the Gothic part of the town hall (to the rear) introduces visitors to the city's history through dioramas. The focus of the exhibition is on the period of the Thirty Years' War, which left traumatic wounds in Rothenburg. Life-sized figures depict the world of mercenaries, aldermen and patricians, including the alchemist Andreas Libavius, who conducts experiments in his laboratory. Historical objects illustrate the life of the burghers during the chaotic years of the war and explain the social structure at that time. In the basement, the curators show three damp, dark cells where the city once incarcerated criminals. The torture instruments in the anteroom secured confessions. The council imprisoned Mayor Heinrich Toppler in the dungeon for two months in 1408. He did not survive his imprisonment and died of thirst in the dungeon.

Until 1803, the fate of Rothenburg was determined by the Inner Council, which consisted of the most influential families in the city. On Walpurgis (April 30) every year, the **patricians** elected a new mayor. From the mid-14th century onwards, the leader of the Outer Council was invited to represent the interests of the craftsmen, but his influence was limited. The law classified him as an assistant without the right to vote. The town was small, the political options were limited, and reelection to the office was the norm.

Jurisdiction in Rothenburg initially rested with the imperial regional court. After the town was declared an Imperial City on May 15, 1274, it exercised high jurisdiction. In the beginning, justice was administered at the Reichshofstatt outside the castle. The battlement between the two towers in the coat of arms refers to the arbour of the court, which was an open hall with twelve seats for the lay judges. The court was responsible for ruling on perjury, theft, robbery, assault and murder. In 1409, the city purchased the Landwehr's regional court, and since then, civil justice has been under the control of the patricians. The place of jurisdiction moved to the town hall in the same year.

▲ The museum shows the city's history during the Thirty Years' War.

Until Bavaria annexed the region in 1803, the interlocking between the legislative, judicial and executive branches was tight. The Inner Council held influence over all three bodies. Patricians also occupied most, if not all, offices in the city. The mayor, master builder and leaders of the guardianship were all recruited from families belonging to this social class. The patricians controlled the tax office and the bailiwick, regulated the market and trade, oversaw the infrastructure and held sway over all church institutions. The power held by the patricians was hereditary. The eldest son followed in his father's footsteps. In short - an oligarchic regime governed Rothenburg.

Historiengewölbe: Marktplatz 1 **Entrance:** Adults 3,50 €, Concessions 2,00 €
Opening Times: Mon - Sun 10.00 - 17.00
Internet: www.meistertrunk.de

The revolt of 1451

Oligarchic structures inevitably lead to corruption due to their interlocking of public and private interests. The fate of Heinrich Toppler best exemplifies the Inner Council's workings. As long as his risky ventures yielded profits, the patricians participated in his endeavours. When Rothenburg lost the conflict with Nürnberg and Würzburg, the council expelled his family from the Landwehr and killed the mayor in 1408. At times, the lower classes rebelled against nepotism and demanded a say. In 1451, after the Second City War, the burghers captured members of the Inner Council and demanded more rights for the craftsmen. However, four years later, the Rothenburger aristocracy regained the upper hand, and the uprising fizzled out. The oligarchic regime ended when Bavaria annexed the region.

Fleisch- und Tanzhaus

Facts & Figures

During the Middle Ages, the burghers celebrated their festivals on the first floor of the half-timbered house behind the Heterichsbrunnen. It stands out with its impressive roof. Here, the people gathered for banquets, music and dancing. Butchers sold meat on the ground floor, and that's how the name came about: Fleisch- und Tanzhaus (House of Meat and Dancing). Until the 18th century, citizens bought sausages in its market hall. Today, the Rothenburger Künstlerbund e.V. exhibits works of art from local artisans; some of their works can be purchased. Historians believe that the complex was constructed at the location of the first town hall, which burned down in 1240. For centuries, the building served as a garment house where the vigilantes kept their uniforms. To this day, the administration of the historical festival uses some rooms as a clothing store.

The Rothenburger Landwehr was organised as a feudal system; farmers were subject to the jurisdiction of their masters. During the Turkish Wars and the epidemics of the 14th and 15th centuries, Rothenburg imposed a heavy tax burden on its subordinates, pushing many farmers and some burghers to the brink of existence. The council levied a tax on livestock and demanded work on the city wall. From 1520, the patricians enforced a land fee for the vineyards. The tax was 25%. Martin Luther's 95 theses, which he had nailed to the entrance of the church in Wittenberg in 1517, resonated with the impoverished population. People studied the Holy Scriptures to find an argument for an uprising in faith - and they did: *"God does not define the social structure, no word about it, we do not have to endure the oppression!"*

In March 1525, the **Peasants' Revolt** swept over Rothenburg. The farm workers banded together. Even the burghers rose up against the Inner Council. Many craftsmen sympathised with the farmers. After the insurgents' initial success, the ruling class responded with might and sent in a professional army. The revolt was brutally suppressed. Soldiers of the Swabian Confederation occupied Franconia, and Markgraf Casimir

▲ Rothenburg exhibits local artists in the Fleisch- und Tanzhaus.

von Ansbach stationed troops in and around Rothenburg. The revolution was crushed veraciously; the sentence for the ringleaders was without mercy.

Moreover, Markgraf Casimir von Ansbach sacked Brettheim and Ohrbach, the villages where the rebellion had started. In Rothenburg, he presided over the trial of the leaders. On June 30, 1525, he passed his verdict. Capital punishment! In total, eighteen agitators were sentenced to death. They were tortured and executed on the Marktplatz - for everyone to see. As a deterrent, their bodies were left to rot for days. Eyewitnesses report that the victims' blood turned the streets dark red.

Location: Marktplatz 1 **Entrance:** Without charge **Internet:** Rothenburger Künstlerbund e.V. on Facebook **Opening Times:** Fri, Sat 14.00 - 20.00, Su 14.00 - 17.00
Käthe-Wohlfahrt: https://www.kaethe-wohlfahrt.com/weihnachtsdorf-rothenburg-ob-der-tauber

The Christmas Museum

No need to celebrate Christmas on midwinter's day! In Rothenburg, romantics enjoy glitter balls, nutcrackers and angels all year round. Opposite the Fleisch- und Tanzhaus, the Käthe-Wohlfahrts-Weihnachtsland shows the wonderful miracle of the birth of Jesus Christ in a museum and introduces Bavaria's Christmas customs. Garlands, nativity figures and Santa Clauses can be purchased all year round. Rothenburg is transformed into a snowy land of fairy tales during Advent: a decorated Christmas tree welcomes visitors on the Marktplatz, and market stalls offer mulled wine and cookies. Another amazing experience is at Obere Schmiedgasse 1, where grumpy teddy bears look for new owners to be cuddled and loved. For the young? For the old? The toys are for everyone to enjoy!

St Jakob

Facts & Figures

The burghers constructed the Gothic Basilica of St Jakob between 1311 and 1484. It is dedicated to the evangelist Saint Jacob, the patron saint of pilgrims. A Holy Blood Relic has attracted believers since 1270. The church dominates the landscape from afar; its monumental towers, 55 and 58 metres tall, rise over the roofs of the townhouses. The building symbolises the self-confidence of an Imperial City and testifies to the prosperity the burghers enjoyed during their golden days. Tilman Riemenschneider's Heilig-Blut-Altar, created in 1505, depicts the Last Supper. The delicate lime wood carving is impressive. The Zwölf-Boten-Altar, a beguiling piece of art created by Friedrich Herlin around 1466, is also worth seeing. The colourful windows, designed around 1400, depict prophets, the life of Mary, and the blood sacrifice of Jesus Christ. A curiosity: the west choir is built above the Klingengasse.

When the Deutscher Ritterorden obtained the Detwanger Church of St Peter und Paul in the Tauber Valley in 1258, the order of knights, founded in 1199 during the Third Crusade, had secured a branch in the Landwehr. In the 13th century, the order took over a chapel in Rothenburg, probably the Heilig-Blut-Kapelle (Holy Blood Chapel), first mentioned in 1278. Around 1270, a drop from the chalice of the Last Supper turned into the blood of Christ and made it to Rothenburg. The people placed the drop in a rock crystal and presented the miracle in a chapel. The exciting news about indulgences quickly triggered a wave of pilgrimages. Since 1505, the capsule has been part of an altar carved by the artist Tilman Riemenschneider.

Rothenburg laid the founding stone for the Church of **St Jakob** at the east choir in 1311. Work on the nave began in 1373 and was completed around 1436. In 1408, the citizens interred the remains of Heinrich Toppler, a former mayor, in the southeast side chapel. The construction of the western section, in which the Holy Blood Relic is kept, was finished in 1471. The church was formally inaugurated in 1484 after over 150 years of construction.

As the work progressed, the city councillors became increasingly involved. By the middle of the 14th century, they financed the project and thus decided the structure. At that time, all cities endeavoured to strengthen their secular power by constructing religious landmarks.

After the Reformation, the church celebrated its first Protestant service in 1544. The new faith enforced a redesign of the House of the Lord, and the galleries were added. In the 19th century, the basilica returned to its original Gothic style. Karl Alexander von Heideloff was in charge of the restoration. The spirit of the city had returned to its traditional roots.

▲ St Jakob rises over the roofs of the old town.

Location: Kirchplatz **Entrance**: Adults: 2,50 €, Concessions: For free
Opening Times: Mon - Sat 10.00 - 18.00, Sunday 11.00 - 18.00
Internet: http://rothenburg-evangelisch.de/pfarrei-st-jakob

The Way of the Pilgrim

St Jakob is dedicated to the patron saint of pilgrims. At the entrance, his aura welcomes all visitors walking along a spiritual path. Rothenburg used to be a stopover along a pilgrimage route to Rome or Santiago de Compostela. The hiking trail *Jakobswanderweg* passed through the city. The purpose of the arduous journey was to obtain indulgence for one's sins. In Rothenburg, a drop from the chalice of the Lord's Supper promised spiritual cleansing. The path from the Tauber Valley to the castle was created to replicate the path Jesus followed on Mount of Olives. The pilgrims could be recognised by their clothing, which included a shell, a pilgrim's staff and a wide-brimmed hat. During their journey, they enjoyed the protection of the Church. In Rothenburg they stayed overnight at the Neue Spital in the neighbourhood Kappenzipfel.

Highlights of the Church of St Jakob

The Church of St Jakob is a striking landmark visible from afar. As a symbol of the settlement, it demonstrates the self-confidence of the patricians and burghers to guard both the worldly and the spiritual prosperity of the Imperial City. A now-dissolved **cemetery** to the east of the choir was once the final resting place of Rothenburgers. Its funeral chapel, the Michaelskapelle, was demolished in 1812, and its altar by Tilman Riemenschneider moved to the Church of St Peter und Paul in Detwang.

At the **entrance** in the southwest of the Gothic church, the statue of a pilgrim awaits the believers. Inside, the basilica demonstrates sober elegance. The **central nave** is connected to the side aisles by a 24-metre-high cross vault.

The monumental **Zwölf-Boten-Altar** in the east choir was created around 1466. The Rothenburg artist Friedrich Herlin, a student of Rogier van der Weyden, designed the paintings. They show scenes from the life of Mary, including the Annunciation, Adoration of the Magi, and the Death of the Virgin. On the left of the Predella, next to Jesus with a globe, the apostle Peter studies the Bible with a pair of medieval glasses. The altar's back features the legend of Saint Jacob. Two bulls drag the saint's body into the city in the left wing. In the background, one identifies Rothenburg's town hall before the fire in 1501. The front of the altar features the crucifixion, accompanied by four angels and six saints, including Saint Jacob (second from the left).

The **choir windows** were designed in the latter half of the 14th century. The central window features prophets from the Old Testament and depictions of the birth of Christ. The northern window is dedicated to the life of Mary, while the southern window refers to the Holy Blood Relic.

The figurative **sacrament niche** (to the left) was created around 1377. It is dedicated to the Eucharist and the Trinity. At the northern corner, near the steps to the choir, the **Archangel Michael** battles a dragon. The sculpture was chiselled around 1462.

The **Maria-Krönungs-Altar** in the north aisle was designed around 1520 by an unknown master from Tilman Riemenschneider's circle. It depicts the coronation of Mary, with the design based on an engraving by Albrecht Dürer. The depiction of Mary's death on the Predella shows a Franconian farmhouse.

According to art historians, the Heilig-Blut-Altar by Tilman Riemenschneider in the West Choir is a stunning masterpiece and the highlight of any tour through the Church of St Jakob. The altar was designed between 1501 and 1505 on the initiative of the Inner Council. The work was intended to give the Holy Blood Relic a dignified setting. The altar is made of lime wood and shows the Last Supper. The gilded cross, dating from around 1270, holds a capsule made of rock crystal that contains a drop from the chalice of the Last Supper.

Tilman Riemenschneider captivates with his delicate work. The figures virtuously bring the characters of the twelve disciples to life. Watch out for Judas, who can be seen with a money bag, and John, who sleeps in Jesus's lap.

▲ St Jakob was a stopover on the pilgrimage route to Rome or Santiago de Compostella.

The City's old High School

Opposite the Church of St Jakob, a three-story building refreshingly stands apart from the medieval atmosphere of the old town: the Alte Gymnasium of Rothenburg - the city's old high school, once a Latin school. The architect Leonhard Weidmann constructed the building in the Renaissance style between 1589 and 1591. The structure is notable for its octagonal tower, with a spiral staircase connecting the floors. In 1703, an exquisite baroque portal with two atlases was added to the building. The citizens of Rothenburg used the spacious attic as a granary and installed a lavish wine cellar in the basement. Today, the building houses a community centre run by the parish. On March 31, 1945, an Allied air raid almost destroyed the Gymnasium. It was meticulously restored after World War II.

⑨ Klostergarten

Facts & Figures

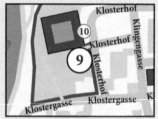

In the 13th century, Rothenburg founded a monastery for Dominican nuns on the northern edge of the old town, where today, the Rothenburg Museum presents the city's history. The former herb garden, surrounded by a protective wall, still exists. This beautiful garden provides a peaceful escape to relax and rejuvenate. In the 16th century, the monastery was dissolved; after the Reformation, the buildings passed on to the city. The serene meadows are framed by trees that offer soothing shade during the summer months. Buzzing bees feast on wildflowers. During World War II, citizens grew vegetables in the garden. Later, it served refugees for recreation. The monastery's garden opened its doors to the public in 1949. It has been a mesmerizing attraction ever since. Locals and visitors alike seek contemplation in this tranquil space. The entrance is without charge.

Two knightly orders and two monasteries protected Rothenburg's spiritual life during the Middle Ages. The **Dominicans** were the first non-knightly order in the city. Lupold von Nordenberg founded the convent in Neusitz. In 1258, it moved to Rothenburg; the nuns were housed in the castle's former farmyard. At Christmas 1265, the city inaugurated the complex. Even the friar Albertus Magnus was present. About twenty years later, the Franciscans settled in town on Herrngasse.

During the Middle Ages, upper-class women had only two options: marriage or convent. The daughters of the lower nobility who could not be married ended in the Dominican convent. The order cared for the city's poor. The monastery served food to those in need through a revolving window. Lay people, known as Konversen, supported the nuns. They were not members of the order but closely affiliated. Donations from burghers and patricians secured the financial stability of the convent. Within, the nuns controlled the daily routine. Life was determined by church law and not city law. The monastery ruled independently and, therefore, remained a nuisance to the Inner Council, which had no power over the daily activities.

▲ The former herb garden of the Dominican convent invites to meditate.

It was not the goal in life to be forced into chastity for all young women who entered the convent. To keep up the morality of the nunnery was a challenge. Rumours have it that the sons of patrician families freely loitered around the building, singing mocking songs beneath the women's bathroom.

The Inner Council repeatedly tried to take charge of the monastery in vain. After the Reformation, the magistrate closed the institution. In 1554, the last nun passed away, and the complex was handed over to the city. Other nuns had left the church early and married their long-term lovers. Freed from their vows, they chose a secular life over a spiritual one.

Location: Klosterhof 5 **Entrance**: without charge
Opening Times: April - October: open during the day, November - March: closed
Literature: Rothenburger Gartenparadiese (Rothenburg Tourismus Service)

Rothenburg's Gravedigger

Rothenburg's gravedigger lived in the outer monastery garden on the northwest corner of the Dominican convent. When the cemetery at the Church of St Jakob was abandoned, the beggars' reeve took over the tower. A water reservoir on the inner wall, the Totenweth, served as a pool to extinguish fires. The building next to it housed a torture chamber. Those curious can see the instruments at the Mittelalterliche Kriminalmuseum, which exhibits them. The beggars' reeve was a lower-ranking official responsible for monitoring the beggars. He ensured compliance with the law regarding alms. In 1562, the city opened a new cemetery with a chapel at the Rödertor. Important Rothenburger families are buried there with beautiful gravestones. The Jewish community had its cemetery on the Schrannenplatz.

Facts & Figures

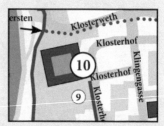

Rothenburg displays its cultural and historical treasures in the former halls of the Dominican convent. As early as the 1870s, the Gewerbeverein (trade association) collected artfully crafted pieces. The exhibits were passed on to the Verein Alt-Rothenburg (an association to study the history of Rothenburg) in 1898, which presented them in the Fleisch- und Tanzhaus. In the 1930s, the museum moved to the convent. The curators present objects from Rothenburg and the Landwehr. The exhibits include sandstone figures, chalices, household altars, and tankards. Liturgical objects from the convent are on display as well. The Sammlung Baumann (Baumann Collection) shows weapons from the Middle Ages, such as swords, guns, helmets, and cannons. Paintings depicting Rothenburg complement the exhibition. The Rothenburger Passion from 1494 presents the story of Jesus's suffering in twelve panels.

When the magistrate took ownership of the Dominican convent after the Reformation, the patricians had no plans to utilise the complex. Only when the **Rothenburg Museum** moved into the premises in 1933 did the facility find a new purpose.

The curators maintain around 20,000 culturally and historically relevant objects from Rothenburg and the Landwehr. Some of which are presented to the public. The exhibits provide valuable insight into the lives of burghers and farmers from the Middle Ages to the present.

Along the cloister, the museum protects numerous sandstone figures from the weather. They once adorned the facades of houses and were replaced by replicates. The seven virtues and seven sins of the Baumeisterhaus are among them.

The historical kitchen of the convent is the oldest surviving commercial kitchen in Germany. The chimney extends across all floors and served as a heating system. Through a revolving door, the nuns distributed food to those in need. Axes, spearheads and bronze swords illustrate the early history of the region. In the section *Judaica*, the curators explain the history of the Jewish community in Rothenburg.

▲ The Rothenburg Museum shows the city's cultural and historical collection.

On the upper floor, the Sammlung Baumann shows weapons from the Middle Ages. In addition to swords, lances and firearms, various armour and helmets are displayed. Objects from everyday life complement the exhibition.

The painting collection from the 19th century shows picturesque city views. At the turn of the century, the British artist Arthur Wasse immortalised Rothenburg and its burghers with his sensitive art. The historical section in the winter refectory illustrates the life of the patricians.

Last but not least, at the museum's entrance, the curators present the tankard that inspired the grotesque farce *Der Meistertrunk*.

Location: Klosterhof 5 **Entrance**: Adults: 5,00 €, Concessions: 3,00 €
Opening Times: daily 9.30 - 17.30, Winter 13.00 - 16.00
Internet: https://www.rothenburgmuseum.de // https://www.alt-rothenburg.de

The Rothenburger Passion

The 12 panels in the convent hall of the monastery show the story of Jesus's suffering. The paintings are executed in tempera on spruce wood and are considered the highlight of the Rothenburg Museum. The well-crafted pictures were created around 1494. Probably the head of the Franciscan monastery at that time, Martinus Schwarz, executed them for the monastery's rood screen parapet. The characters in the paintings have coarse faces; their eyes are piercing, their noses raw. In contrast, Jesus's features appear meditative, melancholic and removed. The Son of God surrenders to what has to happen. The colours are subtle. They reflect the Franciscans' vow to a life of poverty. Unusually, the series of panel paintings begins with Jesus on the Mount of Olives and not with his entry into Jerusalem.

⑪ Klingentor

Facts & Figures

Rothenburg's first city wall stretched up to the Klosterweth; only the gates on Galgengasse and Rödergasse survived, however. The citizens built the Klingenbastei and the fortified Church of St Wolfgang around 1360. The barbican, which once had a drawbridge over the city moat, was added in 1592. The bend in the road within the bastion was designed to prevent the use of battering rams. The Klingentor, which is 37 metres tall, stands out because of its high bay windows. The name comes from the steep slope of the area that drops down into the Tauber Valley, which the Rothenburgers call *Klinge* (blade of a knife). From 1595 onwards, the Bronnenmühle pumped drinking water from the Tauber River to the gate, where it was collected in a water reservoir installed in the tower room. The bronze basin supplied the city's fountains with water.

During the 13th century, Rothenburg's population grew rapidly. The first wall along Judengasse and the old city moat soon became too restrictive. More importantly, new weaponry and better siege tactics required a more defensive wall.

Starting from 1250, Rothenburg began to extend its **city wall**. At first, the burghers surrounded the area with an earthen mound and added a picket fence. Only later did they replace the rampart with a stone wall. From 1315 onwards, documents refer to a second city wall, and from 1327 onwards, there is evidence of taxes being used to finance the maintenance of the facility. By around 1400, the burghers had completed the enclosure, which protected an area of about 38 hectares. The interior was spacious at the beginning and even allowed for gardens. The first city wall remained in operation during the construction of the expansion. The burghers filled in the ditches in the late Middle Ages.

During the Hussite War and the Thirty Years' War, the Inner Council reinforced the fortifications. The patricians built barbicans, added an earth wall around the northwestern part of the city, and organised the defence by section. A kennel made it more difficult for attackers to retreat, and thus,

the enemy's losses increased. However, the northern flank from the Klingentor to the Kummereck remained a weak spot; it was here where Johann Graf von Tilly achieved a decisive breakthrough in 1631 after a gunpowder depository exploded.

Forty-two towers defended the complex. It is worth noting that squared buildings like the Klingentor are older than round towers. The latter were constructed in response to the invention of guns during the 15th century. Builders designed the curved walls to deflect cannon balls; the ammunition was unlikely to hit perpendicular to the wall, the impact was severely weakened, and the structure survived.

▲ The Rothenburgers constructed the Klingentor between 1395 and 1400.

Location Klingentor: Klingengasse 15. No visiting of the building possible.
Opening Times city wall: Anytime **Entrance:** Without charge
Literature: Turmweg-Broschüre (Rothenburg Tourismus Service)

The Strafturm

The Strafturm (penalty tower) is situated between the Rothenburg Museum and the Klingentor on the northwestern side of the fortifications. Along with the Faulturm and the Frauenturm, the tower served as a prison for minor offences. Since 1410, the city used it as a dungeon. The round tower was inserted to ensure a maximum distance of 150 metres between towers. This length was measured based on the range of arrows and bullets. The conical roof was likely added around 1730. The Strafturm has become a popular nesting place for wild birds such as jackdaws, falcons, and swifts. Bird lovers have also spotted bats. Ursula von Seckendorf, the prioress of the Dominican convent, was held as a prisoner in the Strafturm in 1394. The Inner Council attempted to pressure the monastery to enforce a say, but the godly Lady answered with piety.

St Wolfgang

Facts & Figures

The city built the imposing late Gothic fortified Church of St Wolfgang in 1475. It was the church of the shepherds who worshipped the patron saint of their guild at the chapel. A seated figure between the portal and the crucifix shows his image. A battlement leads from the church attic to

the Klingentor, while casemates reinforce the defence to the north. Instead of traditional church windows, there are loopholes to shoot at the enemy. The shepherds fired from the sacristy and the side chapels. A gun base strengthened the defences of the facility. The ribbed star vault above the nave dates back to the Middle Ages. The high altar is dedicated to Saint Wolfgang. In addition, it shows carved figures of Saint Sebastian and Saint Rochus. In the gatehouse, a museum presents Rothenburg's sheep farming and the shepherd's dance. It is open to visitors at irregular hours.

Since the 14th century, Rothenburg had four teams of **watchmen** spread across the city. Two others were stationed at the Maktplatz. Their primary responsibility was to maintain order within the city and defend their section during a siege. Tower guards overlooked the streets at the Klingenturm, Galgenturm, Röderturm, and the town hall tower. In the run-up to the Thirty Years' War, 25 additional guards roamed through Rothenburg and ensured security with sword and lance. Sixteen citizens patrolled along the battlements. After the Prague Defenestration, the council replaced them with 32 full-time guards.

When the army of the Catholic League marched on Rothenburg under Johann Graf von Tilly in 1631, the attackers' victory was inevitable. The city had around 6,000 inhabitants and mobilised 850 armed defenders. The community counted 400 muskets and protected a wall that spanned 3,600 metres - in short - one soldier every five metres guarded the city against the attacking enemy. Additionally, the burghers were not only poorly equipped, they also lacked basic training as soldiers. Given these circumstances, the downfall of the settlement was predictable and only a matter of time.

In particular, the northern flank from the Klingentor to the Kummereck caused great concern, but the city lacked the financial resources to provide additional protection, e.g. ramparts.

By the 17th century, Rothenburg's city wall was no match for the military technology of the time. It only provided a policing role. The guards locked the gates at nightfall, but for financial reasons, the gatekeepers were recruited from the poor who had gotten into trouble through no fault of their own. The defence system controlled pilgrims, carts and passers-by, kept out gangs of robbers, but the walls were no match for a professional army.

▲ At the Church of St Wolfgang the shepherds worshipped God.

Location: Klingentor **Entrance:** Adults 1,50 €
Opening Times: Mon - Sun 10.00 – 16.30
Museum: Opening Times irregular, http://www.schaefertanzrothenburg.de

Rothenburg - an Imperial City

City air is the air of freedom. On May 15, 1274, King Rudolf I proclaimed Rothenburg an Imperial City and granted autonomy. This privilege defined the further development of the community. The city was only subordinate to the king and served no other authority. It was exempt from courts outside the city, and Rothenburg's Central Court became the court of the Landwehr. In the same year, documents testify the first criminal trials. However, the transition from the Middle Ages to modern times reveals the severe disadvantage of a land structured by independent Imperial Cities: Like most other towns, Rothenburg found it challenging to gain influence; the town depended on alliances that threatened its independence. Among others, Nürnberg and Würzburg tried to gain power over Rothenburg.

(13) Battlements

Facts & Figures

Visitors are welcome to explore the northern and eastern parts of the medieval battlements. The parapet provides a glimpse into the defence system of the Imperial City during the Middle Ages. The walk allows to experience the old town from a birds-eye perspective. Forty-two gates and towers line up along the way. Mighty roof structures, cannon bases and a water pipe are to be seen. Hardly any other town preserved the wall as well as Rothenburg: After the Thirty Years' War, the city became impoverished and lacked the financial means to demolish the complex. The population stagnated until the 19th century; no other pressure, such as economic growth, enforced the destruction. Unlike Munich or Heidelberg, there was no enforced city expansion either; no king wanted to turn down the wall to create ample space. In short, the city's poverty ensured the survival of the medieval fortifications to the present day.

High above the ground, an approximately 1½-metre-wide **battlement** runs along the medieval city wall. Brick-lined foundation arches anchor the structure so deeply in the ground that an attacking army could not undermine the defence system. At 14 locations along the wall, covered stairs lead to the battlements. The staircases, primarily located at gate towers, are made of wood. They could be burned down in case attackers entered the city.

The northern section of the city wall between Klingentor and Galgentor runs in a straight line and offers enemies a broad target for any attack. It was here where the army of the Catholic League concentrated its efforts in 1631. The flank is reinforced by three round towers: Pulverturm, Henkersturm and Kummereck. The Pulverturm, formerly known as the Fürbringerturm, was secured with an iron door and served as a storage site for gunpowder. It is thought that the executioner of Rothenburg lived in the Henkersturm. Rothenburg executed death sentences outside the northern city wall. At the Kummereck, citizens once dumped rubble and waste, hence the name. An underground passage connected the spot to the outer wall.

Casemates fortified the Church of St Wolfgang.

At the Rödertor near the Hornburgweg playground, parts of the kennel and the front towers have been preserved. Pictures and documents in the tower room detail the extent of destruction Rothenburg had experienced by the end of World War II.

The urge of nature was taken seriously as well. In the section near the Rossmühle, an opening in the battlement served as a toilet. This opening is still visible.

The control of the city wall was the responsibility of the Outer Council. Two members had to check all city gates every night to ensure the guards were ready for duty.

▲ The northern and eastern parts of the city wall can be walked.

Location: Encircling the city. Staircases are located at the towers. **Entrance:** Without charge **Opening Times:** Accessible at any time **Donation stones:** Stadtkämmerei Rothenburg ob der Tauber, Marktplatz 1, +49 9861 404300, kaemmerei@rothenburg.de

The Restoration of the City Wall

An Allied air raid struck Rothenburg hard on March 31, 1945, causing damage to around a quarter of the city and seven of its towers. In the aftermath of World War II, preservationists sought to rebuild the destroyed areas of the old town. After the currency reform in 1948, a private initiative called for donations in newspapers to finance the restoration. It was possible then to rebuild one metre of city wall for 59 German Marks. The magistrate still honours all donors with a plaque to this day. In 1953, the final section of the battlement was restored, and the Röderturm returned as a lookout tower. Donation stones for preserving the city wall can be obtained from the Rothenburg City Treasurer's Office for €1,200. The donors will be permanently honoured with an inscription of their choosing on the city wall.

Galgentor

Facts & Figures

During the Thirty Years' War, the Galgentor in the east (also called Würzburg Gate because the arterial road to Würzburg runs through here) was the most vulnerable gate in Rothenburg. It is located at the highest point in the city at 438 metres above sea level and was built in 1388. The troops of the Catholic League entered the city through this gate. The mighty tower and the gate to the front are original. After a partial demolition, the city reconstructed the guard house and the customs house according to original blueprints in 1842. In 1849, the builders added two bay windows to increase the picturesque effect of the complex. Parts of the moat and the kennel can be seen in the park adjacent to the gate. The Galgentor got its name from the execution site located outside the city wall on the Köpfleinswiese (meadow of the beheaded).

Towers increase a city's defensive capabilities and, through their gates, provide access to the inside. Rothenburg built the towers on arterial roads, and they made them before the wall was constructed. Customs duty was collected at city gates for any trade at the market or elsewhere. Subsequent additions of entrances suggest that the complex was constructed before the burghers had finished building the city wall. Only towards the end of the construction did the citizens add the bastions to the front of the towers.

After the invention of firearms in the 15th century, towers were built in a round shape. They were more resistant to firing cannons because the ammunition slid along the masonry. Typically, a city constructed its towers at most 150 metres apart, depending on the terrain. During an attack on one section, neighbouring structures could support the defence.

Rothenburg's old towers, such as the Galgentor, rise more than 30 metres above the ground. They rest on a foundation made of humped blocks. The main gate is constructed behind the wall; the front is aligned with the city wall. During the Middle Ages, the inside of smaller towers remained uncovered for defence reasons.

▲ The path of death led through the Galgentor to the execution site outside the city wall.

Wooden stairs led up to the battlements, which could be set on fire as a last resort if the enemy breached the city wall. Bay windows were installed to provide all-round visibility.

Massive wooden gates ensured the city's security at the passages. Small entrances were added; they allowed access only one by one and could easily be defended. Additionally, a trap door secured some gates, such as the Gebsattlertor. A barbican, as seen at the Galgentor, served as a trap yard. Here, the defenders could fire from the upper perimeter at enemies that had breached the first gate. Each entrance is marked with an Imperial Eagle, symbolising that Rothenburg is an Imperial City.

Location: Vorm Würzburger Tor 6 **Entrance**: Without charge
Opening Times: Always accessible
Internet: https://www.rothenburg-tourismus.de/?s=galgentor

The Blood Court at the Galgenplatz

The Galgenplatz (Gallows Square) was located on the Köpfleinswiese (Meadow of the Beheaded) directly outside the Galgentor (Gallows Tower). The last walk of the condemned led along the Galgengasse (Gallows alleyway) and through the Galgentor (Gallows gate). In 1368, Emperor Karl IV granted the Inner Council blood jurisdiction, which enabled the city to exercise the death penalty for severe crimes (adultery, robbery, murder). The court could also call to order any straying ragtag. The Inner Council thus had the executive power to suppress any revolt in the making through criminal proceedings. The patricians mainly took action against the lower nobility and restricted their influence. During the Middle Ages, falsely accusing an innocent was a popular game to eliminate rivals.

Facts & Figures

Rothenburg constructed the Röderturm, 44 metres tall, between 1385 and 1390. The tower was initially open on the side facing the city for defence purposes. The Rödergasse once led to the shooting range on the Brühl and the city's cemetery, established in 1559. The foundation of the tower is made of limestone, while the upper floors are made of sandstone. From 1615 onwards, the city added a bastion that consisted of a double ditch with a drawbridge and archways to the front. A trap yard with a gatekeeper's house was added in the middle. The kennel, which ran parallel to the city wall, survived the rampages of time at the Röderturm. An Allied air raid damaged this part of the wall in 1945. The tower was rebuilt on the initiative of the Verein Alt-Rothenburg. The tower room showcases an exhibition on the bombing of Rothenburg during World War II.

After World War I, Rothenburg became a **stronghold of the National Socialist German Workers' Party** (NSDAP). In the March 5, 1933 election, the region voted 83% in favour of Adolf Hitler. Rothenburg was a fascist town. Antisemitism was widespread. In October 1938, the Rothenburgers expelled the last 17 Jews from the city and destroyed their synagogue on Herrngasse.

The Nazi regime feared an Allied air raid on the medieval city for a long time, and they asked the photographer Alfons Ohmayer to eternalise the streets and houses in photos. On March 31, 1945, it rained bombs - Rothenburg was set on fire, ablaze. What a tragedy! Only months were left until the Nazi regime surrendered. Within two minutes, an American squadron had unloaded its deadly cargo on the medieval city. The blast destroyed about a third of the buildings. The area between the Weißer Turm and the Röderturm was hit extremely hard. About 750 metres of city walls and many towers collapsed. The buildings were faithfully reconstructed after World War II: many stones carved during the Middle Ages were recovered, and only the mortar was manufactured in the 20th century. The Verein Alt-Rothenburg was involved in the reconstruction, and

▲ The tower room shows the destruction of the city after World War II.

the Bayerische Denkmalamt took the lead. Donations from the population made the reconstruction possible. When the Röderturm once again rose over the Landwehr, the association opened the tower for visitors as a viewing platform. The tower room illustrates the destruction of the city during World War II with photos and documents.

In 1948, the Rothenburg city council elected John McCloy as an honorary citizen. The American was Deputy Secretary of State during the war and prevented further Allied air raids on the city. His mother knew Rothenburg and fell in love with its medieval charm. It was her influence on her son that saved the city.

Location: Rödergasse **Opening Times**: Daily 11.00 - 15.00 (April - October)
Internet: https://www.alt-rothenburg.de/roederturm
NSDAP in Rothenburg: http://www.rothenburg-unterm-hakenkreuz.de

1645: The Year of the French

After the Battle of Nördlingen in 1634, where the Swedish troops were defeated, France was prompted to enter the Thirty Years' War and intervene: the Hapsburg Emperor in Vienna must not take advantage. The Austrians must not determine the course of the war. France was a Catholic country, but they entered the war on the Protestant side. Politics outdid religious ideology. On July 7, 1645, the French general Count Henri de Turenne attacked Rothenburg with 3,000 men. He bombarded the city for two days, created a breach between Galgentor and Rödertor, and forced the city into submission. Rothenburg was exhausted by the war and had nothing left to counter the attack. However, the French did not stay long in Rothenburg. The Tauber Valley could not provide support for their troops. They quickly moved on to Mergentheim and Nördlingen.

Facts & Figures

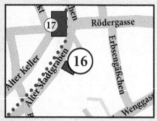

In eleven furnished rooms, the lovingly maintained museum presents the lives of the ordinary people of Rothenburg throughout the centuries. The house was built between 1270 and 1300. It has served as a home and workspace for craftsmen from various industries since the Middle Ages. Weavers, shoemakers, potters, soap makers, print workers and tin casters lived and earned their living in the building at Alter Stadtgraben 26. A 14-metre-deep well supplied the residents with fresh water. The ceilings are low, the beds are short, the floors are made of clay, and the walls are crooked. The kitchen is particularly noteworthy for its open fireplace. The house escaped modernisation after World War II: the owner refused to install a water pipe. He was afraid of electricity, and so unwittingly, the charm of the Middle Ages still howls through the building.

Rothenburg has been hierarchically organised since its founding as a city by the Staufer dynasty. Cooperative associations such as guilds remained prohibited until Bavaria annexed the region in 1803. Even the elevation of Rothenburg to an Imperial City did not bring significant changes to the structure. The patrician class, which emerged from the administrative apparatus in the 13th century, managed to retain the hierarchical structure. The Inner Council only allowed the establishment of brotherhoods to distribute the individual's financial risk among its members, like insurance. The city had, on average, eight brotherhoods, including that of the shepherds.

Craftsmen could acquire citizenship in Rothenburg from 1336 onwards, but the Inner Council controlled their trade throughout the centuries. The city approved becoming a master craftsman and regulated the journeyman, not independent guilds.

New professions emerged, but bakers, butchers, blacksmiths, tanners and dyers remained the dominant occupations in Rothenburg. They supplied the city and the Landwehr. Long-distance trade was unimportant in Rothenburg.

▲ The museum shows the meagre living conditions of the Middle Ages.

Only those who held citizenship were permitted to work as master craftsmen. Citizenship was either inherited, acquired through marriage, or purchased. The reputation of the applicant was crucial. Advocates helped the process. Only legitimate children born to married couples were allowed to become apprentices, and they had to prove their lineage.

Most craftsmen used to live and work in their own homes with their families. Control over the quality of their work was strict as the city had to defend its reputation. The citizens were also responsible for the security of Rothenburg. They had to maintain their section of the city wall and protect it during sieges.

Location: Alter Stadtgraben 26 **Entrance:** Adults 3.00 € Concessions 1.50 €
Opening Times: Easter - October 11.00 - 17.00
Internet: www.alt-rothenburger-handwerkerhaus.de

The Gerlachschmiede

Visitors can find Rothenburg's old blacksmith shop at the Rödertor next to the city wall. The half-timbered house, which is well worth seeing, stands out thanks to its steep roof gable and its decorative facade. Allied air raids destroyed Rothenburg during World War II, and the Gerlachschmiede was not spared, but it could be rebuilt in 1951. The front of the historicizing replica is adorned with a coat of arms showing a crowned snake with a hammer and pliers. It was designed in 1950 by the portrait and landscape painter Georg Gerlach. The graceful little garden covered by the upper floor is enticing. The Gerlachschmiede, as it is called, remained in operation until 1967. This is where the city shod its horses. The house is in private hands and not open to the public.

Facts & Figures

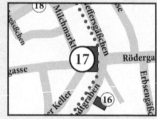

The Röderbogen with its pointed tower and picturesque clock separates Hafengasse from Rödergasse. The passage was part of the first city wall, built from 1172 onwards. The arch is the oldest surviving structure in the city. The border to Rothenburg's old town on the side of the Marktplatz runs here. As usual in the 12th century, the accompanying Markusturm is to the side. Storks nest on its top in summer. The hipped roof was added later. Battlements and embrasures testify to its defensive character. The building on the corner of Rödergasse and Pfeifersgäßchen is now a hotel. In the Middle Ages, it served as a customs house. The buildings around the simple Renaissance fountain were added in the 15th century. At Easter, the burghers decorate the fountain colourfully with painted eggs. It then becomes a popular target for romantic photoshoots.

In the year 1415, during the Council of Constance, the Bohemian theologian Jan Hus was burned alive at the stake as a heretic, but the dispute he started remained unresolved. In 1420, Pope Martin V threatened Bohemia with a crusade. The ecclesiastical argument risked to end in war. During the conflict, the Hussites launched retaliatory attacks. The riders even attacked Bavaria, looting settlements for weapons and food. As a result, Rothenburg strengthened its defence system from 1430 onwards. The city built a kennel and outer walls, added the Sterntürme and the Faulturm, expanded the bastions and protected the Rothenburger Landwehr with an earth wall. Last, the Inner Council strengthened the 62-kilometre-long Landwehr with hedges and bushes, and along the trading arteries, they built watchtowers.

The **Hussite War** never reached Rothenburg, and some historians believe that the fortification of the Landwehr were meant to reinforce border policing. The patricians wanted to make it more difficult for robber bands to smuggle their loot, such as cattle and carts, out of Rothenburg's territory.

The attacks from Bohemia reached Hof, Bayreuth and Sulzbach. From

▲ Storks nest on top of the Markusturm in summer to ensure Rothenburg's offspring.

1430 onwards, the Hussite military campaign concentrated on Silesia, Brandenburg and the Upper Palatinate. Parts of Upper Franconia were also affected, but Rothenburg was never under siege.

The end of the raids came in 1434 with the defeat of the radical units in the Battle of Lipan. Things calmed down in Rothenburg, but the citizens had to meet their debt. The defensive wall was expensive and had to be paid for in taxes and services. The burghers revolted. After the Second City War in 1451, the Outer Council enforced a constitutional change to have a say, but the political uprising did not last long, and the patricians quickly regained power.

Location Röderbogen: Rödergasse 1 **Entrance:** Without charge
Stadtarchiv: Milchmarkt 2, Opening Times: Tues, Thur 8.00 - 12.00, 13.00 - 16.00
Internet: https://www.rothenburg.de/stadtportrait/stadtarchiv

The City Archive in the Büttelhaus

At Milchmarkt 2, next to the Markusturm, Rothenburg holds the written documents of its history in the former Büttelhaus. The first city wall once ran along the building, and Rothenburg's prison was here until 1844. The oldest texts kept in the archives date from 1241. The bishop of Würzburg had written letters to Lupold von Nordenberg. The city used to store these documents first in the Church of St Jakob and later at the town hall. Unfortunately, many historical writings were lost during a fire in 1501. When Bavaria annexed Rothenburg in 1803, the city had to transfer state-relevant documents to the Reichsarchiv München. As a result, only around 4,500 official books remained in Rothenburg, mainly containing administrative files, invoices, registration cards and the records of the registry office.

⑱ Kapellenplatz

Facts & Figures

The first Jewish community in Rothenburg with up to 500 believers settled around the former Milchmarkt on Kapellenplatz during the 13th century. With the black death arriving in the Landwehr in the 14th century, the Jews were forced out of the city. The synagogue was located on

Kapellenplatz. The burghers converted the building into a Lady Chapel around 1404 and demolished it in 1805. Rothenburg also used the former two-story high Talmud Torah as a spiritual house. A hospice next to it looked after the poor and sick in the city. The Jews used to celebrate festivities in a dance house at the Weißer Turm. In addition to a matzo baker and a butcher, the Jewish community also had a medical doctor, a teacher and a Rabbi. The Renaissance-style Seelenbrunnen from 1626, the fountain in the centre, which dominates the square, is reminiscent of the former hospice for the poor.

The first **Jewish community** in Rothenburg settled around the scenic Kapellenplatz in the 13th century. Documents from 1180 mention the first Jew in the city, Samuel Biscoph. At the transition to the High Middle Ages, around 10% of the population in Rothenburg was Jewish. At that time, Christians were prohibited from lending money at interest, and so a city needed Jews to secure the financing of construction projects and military adventures. The Christians soon called them usurers - a peaceful integration of the different population groups was impossible.

During the time of the Holy Roman Empire, the Jewish community was granted protection by the king (Servi camerae regis), but they had to pay a high tax for this privilege. Although they were assured of the safety of life and property and were allowed to practice their religion freely, they still faced frequent attacks. In 1215, the 4th Lateran Council made it mandatory for Jewish citizens to wear a Jewish hat and a yellow ring on their clothing as identification. Additionally, the council prohibited interfaith marriages. The final step towards the exclusion of the Jews from city life was completed. The dress code was later reaffirmed by a Rothenburg council mandate in 1511.

It is not surprising that Jews were repeatedly persecuted. During the Rintfleisch Pogrom in 1298, the Rothenburgers murdered the entire Jewish community - around 500 citizens. The Jews had fled to the Imperial Castle, barricaded there, but could not withstand the siege that followed.

The Jewish community had to endure many violent attacks between 1336 and 1342. After the plague epidemic of 1348/49, the Rothenburgers forced them out of the city, called them poisoners of the wells, and many were murdered. For about 30 years, no Jew lived in the region. It was not until 1375 that documents mention a Jewish community again. It emerged along Judengasse.

▲ The Seelenbrunnen at the Kapellenplatz reminds of the former hospice for the poor.

Location: Kapellenplatz **Entrance:** Without charge **Opening Times:** Always accessible **Internet:** https://www.juedische-allgemeine.de/unsere-woche/wo-rabbi-meir-wohnte Watch out for the section *Judaika* at the Rothenburg Museum (room 10).

Rabbi Meir ben Baruch

When Rabbi Meir ben Baruch lived in Rothenburg in the middle of the 13th century, the Jewish community experienced a joyful cultural heyday. The Rothenburg Museum tells the story of his life. At Kapellenplatz 5, a bronze plaque commemorates the wise master born in Worms in 1215. Rabbi Meir ben Baruch studied in Würzburg and Paris, where King Ludwig IX called upon him to defend the Talmud. When he finally settled in Rothenburg, he gathered a lively community around him. His many students affectionately called him *MaHaRaM*. The scholar worked at the Tauber River for 40 years. His writings provide valuable insight into the everyday life of the community and the city. Despite his success, he emigrated in 1286, was arrested and died in captivity in 1293.

Weißer Turm

Facts & Figures

The Weißer Turm, also known as the inneres Galgentor, is a 33-metre tall city gate of the first city wall. The passage was built at the end of the 12th century. It separates Georgengasse from Galgengasse. The roof, with its elaborate finish, was added around 1730. After the city expanded in the 13th

and 14th centuries, the council decided to preserve the tower. The Jewish dance house at Georgengasse 17 was once situated nearby. The half-timbered house was destroyed during an Allied air raid in 1945, but Rothenburg rebuilt the defence structure after World War II. In the little garden directly at the entrance to the Weißer Turm, a memorial plaque commemorates the expulsion of the Jews during the Nazi regime. Ten tombstones from the 14th century, incorporated into the wall, refer to Rothenburg's Jewish community in the Middle Ages.

After the Thirty Years' War, Rothenburg became dormant until the late 19th century. It was then that the city officials realised the potential of tourism as a source of income. During the Coalition Wars, **Bavaria** was an ally of Napoleon and annexed the region around Rothenburg on September 2, 1802. After the German mediatisation in 1803, large parts of Franconia were placed under the administration of Munich. Only the west of the Landwehr went to what is now Baden-Württemberg. Once Bavaria had risen to a kingdom on January 1, 1806, Rothenburg's independence as an Imperial City ended.

During the reign of King Maximilian I, Bavaria attempted to pay off Rothenburg's debts by selling land along the city wall, but the magistrate defended the town's historic structure and prevented the fortifications from being demolished. Secularisation affected Rothenburg as well. Many art objects were sold, and the city's archive was transferred to Munich. Rothenburg is located in the far northern part of the country, away from Bavaria's capital, and the officials had no interest in promoting the region's economy. It was not until the founding of Germany in 1871 that a gentle wave of industrialisation reached the Landwehr.

The patricians who had controlled the fate of Rothenburg were replaced by Bavarian officials who now defined all aspects of life from afar: A new system of relief for the poor, a fair legal structure, mandatory education, and a pension scheme were introduced. The reformer Maximilian Graf von Montgelas centralised the administration in Munich and spearheaded the reforms throughout the country. The people of Rothenburg experienced the loss of independence and the state's tutelage like bloodletting. This mood has shaped the relationship between Rothenburg and Bavaria ever since. It is still felt to this day.

▲ The Weißer Turm at the Galgengasse was part of the first city wall.

Dürerhaus: Georgengasse 15 **Opening Times**: Mon - Sun 14.00 – 20.00
Entrance: Adults: 2.50 € Concessions: Without charge
Internet: www.grafikmuseum-rothenburg.de

The Dürerhaus Grafikmuseum

Anyone interested in etchings will discover a surprise in the Dürerhaus Grafikmuseum at the Weißer Turm. The artist Ingo Domdey, the owner and curator of the museum, has collected high-quality intaglio prints for many decades and presents them in his museum. The exhibition shows engravings by the artists Albrecht Dürer, Rembrandt van Rijn, Francesco de Goya, Munch and Pierre-Auguste Renoir. Contemporary artists can also be studied: Hrdlicka, Fuchs, Janssen, Richter and Kneffel, amongst others. The museum encourages creativity and offers printing workshops. Visitors can learn the technique under the guidance of the museum. Lectures complement the collection. The Edition Rothenburger Series introduces young upcoming talents to a broad audience. The initiative has been a springboard for some careers.

Facts & Figures

Starting from 1375, Jews returned to Rothenburg and settled along Judengasse until the burghers expelled them in 1520. The street runs along the former moat of the first wall, which was filled in when the expansion was completed. In the 13th century, the path was still outside the inner wall. Historians have found evidence of the first wall at Judengasse 14. Dendrochronological studies reveal that the oldest house in the alley was built around 1399. Jews and Christians lived side by side along that street. The second Jewish community was not a ghetto. However, the rights of Jews were subordinate to those of Christians. During World War II, the Judengasse remained undamaged. Recently, archaeologists found evidence of Jewish life during renovations and excavations, which the curators present at the Rothenburg Museum.

The Rothenburgers had expelled the Jews of the Landwehr after the plague of 1348/49. However, they returned to the city around 1375 and established a **second Jewish quarter** at the Judengasse. Once again, they were under attack and had to defend themselves. For them to gain protection from persecution, Mayor Heinrich Toppler imposed additional taxes on Jews. Partially, these taxes financed the construction of the second city wall, and thus, the enlargement of the city is also a testament to Rothenburg's Jewish past.

Twelve half-timbered houses were built along Judengasse during the 15th century, which gained its name in 1377. Some buildings have survived to this day. The round arches on doors (Judengasse 15/17) are reminiscent of the tablets of the Ten Commandments. Judengasse 10 houses a two-metre-deep mikveh (immersion bath), which was used for ritual ablutions. It is believed that the building served as a matzo bakery. There was a butcher shop two houses further down and a Jewish school at Judengasse 19. At the corner to Deutschherrngasse, archaeologists discovered everyday objects, including a water basin with a jug.

The Jewish cemetery at Schrannenplatz was established around

▲ Along the Judengasse, a Jewish community was established during the 15. century.

1339. From 1407 onwards, a synagogue preached the word of Yahweh there.

During the Reformation, the radical activist Johannes Teuschlein railed against the Israelites and in 1519, the Inner Council decided that all Jews had to leave the city. About a year later, the last six Jewish families fled the Landwehr.

No Jew lived in Rothenburg for almost 300 years. Only when Bavaria annexed Franconia with the help of Napoleon was their right to settle secured. The emancipation edict had made it possible in 1817. In 1871, the Jews achieved the status of citizens. On paper, their rights and duties were, from now on, equal to those of Christians. The reality was different, however.

Location: Judengasse **Entrance:** Without charge **Opening Times:** Always accessible
Literature: Oliver Gussmann: Jüdisches Rothenburg ob der Tauber
Hilde Merz: Zur Geschichte der mittelalterlichen Jüdischen Gemeinde in Rothenburg

The Coemeterium Judaeorum

The Jewish cemetery at Schrannenplatz was established around the year 1339. The burghers called the place Coemeterium Judaeorum. After the Jews had returned to Rothenburg at the end of the 14th century, they constructed a synagogue in 1407. At Schrannenplatz 15, an inscription refers to the Jewish cemetery. During the expulsion of the Jews at the beginning of the 16th century, the citizens looted the synagogue and converted the location into a Christian cemetery. The curators of the Rothenburg Museum present some of the remaining gravestones from that time. The city council tore down the former synagogue in 1561 and used the stones to build a chapel at the Rödertor. The remains of the Jews were buried elsewhere, in a place that none recorded, and the people happily forgot.

Burggarten, Kappenzipfel
and Tauber Valley

Insiders know ...

Stroll through the Gardens
Rothenburg is a city of flowers. Bushes and fruit trees thrive everywhere. The Burggarten offers a beautiful view of the Tauber Valley, and the Leyk's Lotus Garden entices with the charm of Asia.

About Executioners and Witches
At the Mittelalterliche Kriminalmuseum, the good old days present themselves from their gruesome side. Interrogation, torture and beheading were horrifying companions of the Middle Ages. Good nerves are required!

Adventure Parks for Children's Souls
Rothenburg built playgrounds along the outer city wall. Wild nature surrounds the seesaws, climbing frames and sandboxes; the adventures climb trees at the Rothenburger Kletterwald.

About the Poor at the Hospice
The Neue Spital in the Kappenzipfel once cared for the poor and sick. Today, Rothenburg pampers its elderly with lush vegetation. The Stöberleinsbühne is the perfect place for a picnic.

Hiking along the Tauber River
The Tauber River shows the best side of the Landwehr: wild waters, mills, lush meadows, a little castle and a chapel! Tilmann Riemenschneider's engravings in Detwang are the highlight.

Rothenburg Celebrates
The Tauber Festival is Germany's answer to Glastonbury. The backdrop of the city is just stunning. Music, dancing and a playful atmosphere fire up the days. Open air at its finest!

About Winemakers and Wine Bars
The Landwehr is committed to the high quality of the region's wine. Numerous winemakers offer tours around their vineyards. One has to try the lifeblood.

The Best View of Rothenburg
Already Matthäus Merian the Elder captured the best glance on Rothenburg. One has the city's most beautiful view from the Rothenburger Kletterwald or the former ski jump.

◄ At the Kobolzeller Tor, one finds the most recent part of the city wall.

(21) Herrngasse 82

(22) Order of Franciscans 84

(23) Burgtor 86

(24) Burggarten 88

(25) Blasiuskapelle 90

(26) Kriminalmuseum 92

(27) St Johannis 94

(28) Plönlein & Kobolzeller Tor 96

(29) Siebersturm 98

(30) Kappenzipfel 100

(31) Neues Spital 102

(32) Rossmühle 104

(33) Reichsstadthalle 106

(34) Spitaltor 108

(35) Evangelische Tagungsstätte . . . 110

(36) Tauber Valley 112

(37) Doppelbrücke 114

(38) Kobolzeller Kapelle 116

(39) Topplerschlösschen 118

(40) St Peter und Paul in Detwang . . 120

(41) Rothenburg-View 122

A mermaid decorates the
fountain on Herrngasse ▶

The *Herrngasse* once connected Rothenburg's castle with the Marktplatz. Many patricians settled along this artery during the Middle Ages. Here, the *Franciscan Church* awaits the faithful with sober beauty.

Visitors pass through the Burgtor to enter the *Burggarten*. In the 12th century, the Staufer dynasty built a fortress overlooking the Tauber Valley. It was a stronghold to secure their reign. An earthquake demolished the structure in the 14th century. In its place, a garden presents calm tranquillity today. The spot provides a beautiful view of the meadows along the Tauber Valley and offers some enchanting locations for romantic photoshoots.

At the *Mittelalterliche Kriminalmuseum*, Rothenburg displays the dark side of the good old days: the depictions of torture and executions are horrifying.

The *Order of St John* settled in Rothenburg in the 12th century. They ran a simple hospital and accommodated pilgrims to Rome or Santiago de Compostella.

At the *Plönlein*, Rothenburg shows off its most romantic side. The postcard motif made the city famous. The *Siebersturm* separates the old town from the *Kappenzipfel*. In this tranquil neighbourhood, the *Neue Spital* cared for the sick and poor.

The *Rossmühle* was once a pumping station that brought water from the Tauber River into the city. Today, the building serves as a youth hostel. With the *Reichsstadthalle*, the town offers a popular venue for meetings, seminars and conferences.

Those interested in taking a walk along the Tauber River will leave the city through the *Spitaltor*. It is the most impressive bulwark of the enclosure.

The *Evangelische Tagungsstätte* was once a luxury spa hotel. The complex has been under the wings of the Protestant church since 1978. Interested may visit the garden. Numerous paths lead along the Tauber River across the Valley. Meadows invite strollers to dream and beer gardens to have a rest. The magistrate built the *Doppelbrücke* in the 14th century. The bridge allowed traders to cross the Tauber River safely, even during storms. The Peasants' Revolt raged at the *Kobolzeller Kapelle* in 1525. The burghers destroyed all statues and paintings at that time.

The *Topplerschlösschen* is the visible attempt of the former mayor Heinrich Toppler to rise from the rank of a patrician to the status of nobility. Beautiful fruit trees frame the country estate. The Taubertal Festival takes place every year at the nearby Eiswiese. An impressive altar by Tilmann Riemenschneider awaits visitors in the Church of *St Peter und Paul* in Detwang. A final glance at Rothenburg from the former ski jump is the most graceful way to say goodbye to a visit to Rothenburg.

Facts & Figures

The Herrngasse is Rothenburg's artery of power. It connected the now-destroyed castle with the town hall on the Marktplatz, where the Inner Council decided on the future. Around the fountain, erected in 1595 in the late Renaissance style, the citizens held a horse and livestock market. A

mermaid with two fishtails sits atop the column. She wears a crown and presents a wand like a Queen. During the Reichsstadt-Festtage, the organizers recreate the baker's baptism there. In former times, if bakers were caught cheating by baking rolls too small or stretched, the burghers would immerse them in cold water - a punishment that could lead to death. Herrngasse was a preferred residential area for the patricians in the Middle Ages. Numerous Inner Council members resided along the avenue. They designed their villas with a sense of comfort and placed their gardens in the inner courtyard, away from the smelly street.

From the very beginning, the **patricians** determined the fate of Rothenburg. They alone held the seats in the Inner Council, appointed the mayor and made all important decisions. The oligarchical government took shape during the Staufer dynasty. In the High Middle Ages, the patrician class comprised individuals working as Imperial Ministeriales. Unlike in other cities such as Nürnberg, Lübeck or Köln, the ruling families of Rothenburg were hardly involved in long-distance trade - they were administrators. Many rose to power as former royal servants rather than entrepreneurs, and over time, they gradually strengthened their influence in the city and Landwehr.

A cooperative spirit like in Amsterdam never developed. Unsurprisingly, Rothenburg prevented guilds from being established until the 19th century. Entrepreneurial ambition that reached beyond the Landwehr never developed in Rothenburg. The city's strategy was to follow in the footsteps of the fathers, honour tradition, protect what was generated by previous generations and not seek new opportunities. Preserving wealth and not taking risks is the Franconian way of life.

After the Thirty Years' War, Rothenburg was ignored by the rest of

▲ Along Herrngasse, Rothenburg's wealthy patricians settled.

Europe. The city's enormous debt was a bitter pill to swallow for any foreign power seeking to conquer the impoverished region.

Rothenburg reached the peak of its ambitions during the 14th century under the leadership of Heinrich Toppler. With his influence, the city's standing in southern Germany grew. When Toppler was defeated, the town remembered tradition and returned to raising sheep, growing wine, and avoiding taking any risk.

Since then, Rothenburg has missed out on most new cultural inventions. Only through tourism did the burghers discover a new source of income to sustain their economy.

Location: Herrngasse **Entrance:** Without charge **Opening Times:** Always accessible
Märchenzauber: https://stadtmarketing-rothenburg.de/maerchenbummel
Reiterlesmarkt: https://www.rothenburg-tourismus.de/veranstaltungen/weihnachtsstadt

Winter Fairy Tale Rothenburg

In November, Rothenburg turns into a fairy tale land. Poets and artists take the city on a magic tour and enchant the children with captivating fantasies. It is time for the Rothenburger Märchenzauber. Concerts, exhibitions and poetry readings bring the world of myths and legends to life. Anyone strolling the dark alleys at night will believe to have arrived at a long-gone paradise. During Advent, the Rothenburger Reiterlesmarkt looks back on 500 years of tradition. The highlight of the quiet time is the performance of the Reiterle. Once a messenger from another world who rode through the air with the souls of the dead, he now opens the Christmas market; he parades through town with children holding lights in a long chain and singing, accompanied by wind instruments, trumpets and angels.

(22) Order of Franciscans

Facts & Figures

The Franciscan Church is the oldest place of worship in Rothenburg. The order settled in the city around 1281 when the first monks arrived from neighbouring Schwäbisch Hall. The early Gothic church was consecrated in 1309. Its roof once touched the second city wall. In the simple

three-aisled nave, an early work by Tilman Riemenschneider depicts the stigmatisation of Saint Francis of Assisi. The Rothenburger Passion, displayed in the Rothenburg Museum, was created for the rood screen separating the monks' choir from the laity's nave. The interior impresses with its simplicity. Numerous tombstones from Rothenburg patrician families cover the floor. The remains of the knight Dietrich von Berlichingen are buried in a separate tomb. He was Götz von Berlichingen's grandfather. The Reformation dissolved the monastery in 1548, and the church has served the Protestants since 1871.

At the end of the 13th century, the **Franciscans** became the fourth order to settle in Rothenburg after the Johanniter (Order of St John), the Deutschherren and the Dominicans. They wisely settled in the immediate vicinity of the ruling patricians on Herrngasse: "It is easier to beg for alms from the rich than from the poor." The founding of the monastery led to tensions. The citizens wanted to limit the monastery's size, and King Rudolf I had to mediate the dispute.

When the seeds of the Reformation sprouted in the early 16th century, the Franciscans were divided in their opinions. Some saw in Martin Luther the longed-for renewer of Christianity; some condemned his movement as heretical nonsense. In Rothenburg, the Franciscan Johannes Schmid defended the new teachings. Many supported him, like Johannes Teuschlein and Kaspar Christian. However, the councillors remained loyal to the Catholic Church at that time, so the tension grew into an explosive mixture of sociopolitical dimensions. Like Salzburg, many craftsmen and farmers in Rothenburg joined the new faith despite the lead of the patricians - a way to revolt. The Reformation provided theological arguments for the Peasants' Revolt of 1525.

▲ The simplicity of the Franciscan Church once knocked at the conscience of the patricians.

On February 26, 1544, the balance of power shifted suddenly. On that day, the Inner Council decided to introduce the Protestant faith and prohibited the Franciscans from preaching. The monastery was dissolved, and its property placed under the control of the Dominican order, which by then only existed as a legal umbrella run by the patricians.

In 1548, the Franciscan monastery was handed over to the city. The complex served as a Latin school, a retirement home and a warehouse for salt. The monastery has been under the control of the Protestant Church since 1871. Recently, in 2021/22, the building underwent extensive renovations.

Location: Herrngasse **Entrance**: Without charge **Opening times**: Fri - Sun: 14.00 - 16.00
Internet: http://rothenburg-evangelisch.de/unsere-kirchen/franziskanerkirche
Literature: Johannes Rau: Denkmal des Ewigen in der Zeit

Pope Francis in Rothenburg

The Argentinian Jorge Mario Bergoglio, who became Pope Francis in 2013, was born in Buenos Aires in 1936. He studied German at the Goethe-Institut Rothenburg (Herrngasse 17) from August 4th to October 2nd, 1986. The then 50-year-old lived in a small nine-square-metre room at Judengasse 27. He was known to be very polite and tidy, interested in the history of the city, and celebrated masses silently. He diligently learned German, although with a porteño accent. However, little remains of his stay. The house where he lived in Judengasse was cleared out, and his room was used otherwise. The Goethe-Institut, close to the Franciscan Church, was closed at the end of 2005. The facility had become unprofitable, and the management could not maintain the picturesque school.

Facts & Figures

The Burgtor is the tallest tower in Rothenburg. It was built after an earthquake in the 14th century. The citizens added the front gate around 1460 and the northern customs house around 1596. A moat with a drawbridge strengthened the fortification. The bridge's grooves can still be identified at the tower. A small door on the inner gate allowed latecomers entry at night. The wood of the door was harvested around 1555. The bulwark is adorned with Rothenburg's coat of arms and an Imperial Eagle. North of the Burgtor, where the castle wall leads into the city wall, the Schneiderstürmle (tower of the tailors) rises at the Burgeck (corner at the castle). There, the tailors guarded their section of the wall. In the 13th century, the imperial court met at an arbour on the square in front of the Burgtor. The Rothenburg coat of arms depicts the early structure between the two towers.

On the mountain spur above the Tauber Valley close to the village Detwang, an **Imperial Castle** was built under the Staufer dynasty, located on the current site of the Burggarten. The fortress was built by King Konrad III from 1142 onwards. During the 12th century, a settlement developed east of the fortress, from which the city of Rothenburg emerged. A document mentions burghers for the first time in 1227, a city seal is known by 1239, the settlement became a Civitas in 1241, a city coat of arms appears in 1269, and in the same year, documents mention a Rothenburg council.

The first fortifications were constructed in 1172. The inner city wall stretched in a semicircle along Judengasse and the old city moat around the Marktplatz. Markusturm and Weißer Turm date from this period. They were built around the year 1200. At that time, an earth wall with palisades served as the enclosure, later replaced by a stone wall. It stretched over 1,400 metres and covered an area of 13 hectares. The complex was demolished in the late Middle Ages after the second city wall had been built and the ditches were filled in. The second Jewish quarter emerged along the Judengasse shortly after.

▲ The Burgtor is the border between the city and the former fortress.

The Staufer dynasty ended after the death of King Friedrich II in 1250. However, the Imperial Ministeriales retained their power, amongst them Lupold von Nordenberg, who kept his influence during the uncertain times of the interregnum. The Dominican convent was founded thanks to his vibrant initiative.

When Rudolf von Hapsburg was elected king in 1273, ending the turmoil of the interregnum, he immediately sought to regain influence over the lost territories. A year later, he certified Rothenburg's rights as an Imperial City - free and independent. The settlement became self-controlled but remained under the king's authority.

Location: Herrngasse 38 **Entrance**: Without charge **Opening times**: Always accessible
Internet: https://www.rothenburg-tourismus.de
Grafenburg: Jörg Faßbinder: Die mittelalterliche Befestigung auf dem Essigkrug.

The Grafenburg

Historians believe that the Grafen von Komburg built a fortification around 1080, approximately 70 years before the Staufer dynasty constructed an Imperial Castle. The complex was possibly located above the Kobolzeller Kirche at the Essigkrug (meaning: vinegar jug - the wine in this area was sour) on the current site of the Neue Spital. It was part of the Detwang parish. Graf Burkhard, who died in 1116, converted his father's complex in Komburg into a Benedictine monastery. Heinrich, the fourth brother, allegedly built a new castle above the Tauber River. This fortress might have given Rothenburg its name. However, there are no remains left of the fortress, and its existence is disputed among historians. The reuse of the area since the High Middle Ages has erased all traces, and the existing evidence is questionable.

㉔ Burggarten

Facts & Figures

In 1142, Konrad III of the Staufer dynasty, proclaimed king four years earlier, commissioned a fortress 60 metres above the Tauber Valley. It consisted of residential buildings, a hall and a chapel. Only parts of the wall and the Blasiuskapelle have survived, however. In 1356, an earthquake

destroyed the complex. The Rothenburgers used some of the stones to construct the second city wall. The tranquil garden has welcomed strollers since 1864. The green oasis is adorned with eight sandstone figures. They show personifications of the four seasons and the four elements. The view of the surrounding Tauber Valley is breathtaking. A monument commemorates Heinrich Toppler, who passed away in 1408. An inscription reminds visitors that Rothenburg is twinned with the French town Athis Mons. The castle garden is most romantic in the evening.

The **Burggarten** is a serene landscape garden that offers a stunning view over the Tauber Valley. The open space provides visitors a good overview of the city's geographical location and a glimpse how the surrounding Landwehr is used agriculturally.

The citizens established the garden at the former castle in 1864. As early as 1859, the Schillingsfürst court gardener had presented an attractive blueprint for the park's overall design. In the 16th century, the Rothenburgers planted fruit trees and flowerbeds on the mountain spur. In the early 20th century, merchants sold tobacco products, ice cream and souvenirs in the garden, promoting tourism in the region. In 1964, the city installed a lighting system, and the magistrate allowed access during the evening hours.

The use of the area was based on the interests of the local residents: the upper middle class sought a garden for relaxation, the working class demanded agricultural land to grow fruit and vegetables, and the tourism industry, which had been established by the 20th century, advocated a design that would appeal to foreign visitors.

Rothenburg and its Landwehr were dominated by agriculture until

▲ A castle rose at today's **Burggarten** until the 14th century.

the 20th century. The citizens even grew vegetables in the old town. At the turn of the century, farmers kept livestock within the wall. The difference in class was reflected in the management: While the patricians had extensive gardens to the back of their houses, the middle class had to lease plots of land in front of the city wall. They were between 8 to 75 square metres in size. The city regulated the cultivation of vegetables and fruit trees, of course. The council even administered the use of manure for fertilisation. The allotments survived until the 20th century. Seed traders were known in Rothenburg since the 17th century. They required a concession, too.

Location: Burggarten **Entrance:** Without charge **Opening Times:** Always accessible
Internet: https://rothenblog.blogspot.com/2018/12/burggarten-rothenburg-ob-der-tauber.html
The Jews in Rothenburg: http://www.judengemeinde.de/pc/de/rathaus.html

A working group promoting Jewish history

Promoting awareness of the history of the Jewish community in Rothenburg, encouraging cultural exchange, and fostering mutual understanding between different religions are not inventions of the post-war years. The Arbeitsgemeinschaft für jüdische Geschichte (Working Group for Jewish History) was founded by the Jewish community in 1878. The Constitution of 1871 had granted freedom of religion and the right to settle. The Jewish community acquired a building at Herrngasse 21 (corner of Heringsbronnengässchen) and converted it into a synagogue. The prayer house had a school and an apartment for the teacher on the upper floor. By 1910, the community had grown to 100 members. Unfortunately, any Christian-Jewish sympathy was violently oppressed by the Nazi regime.

(25) Blasiuskapelle

Franconia was Germany's stronghold of **National Socialism**. Two years after Adolf Hitler had founded the NSDAP in Munich's Hofbräuhaus, elementary school teacher Julius Streicher established a local group in Nürnberg. In April 1919, their people's militia took violent action against left-wing activities in Rothenburg. The radical association had 300 members. The local group NSDAP Rothenburg Stadt was formed in 1927. During the Deutsche Tage (German Days), the right-wing extremists propagated ethnic ideologies and systematically bombarded all villages in the area with antisemitic slogans. Their gangs of brown thugs roamed the streets. Adolf Hitler's propaganda machine fell on fertile ground in Franconia from the very beginning.

Konstantin Freiherr von Gebsattel, owner of Gebsattel Castle within sight of Rothenburg, had been chairman of the anti-Semitic Deutschvölkischer Schutz- und Trutzbund (a right-wing federation) since April 30, 1920. As early as 1913, he called in a memorandum for a radical, anti-Semitic solution. In 1920, the Nazis smeared swastikas on the synagogue and the houses of Jewish citizens in Rothenburg. The Tauber Valley was a proud showcase for the National Socialists.

From 1933 onwards, the actions took another level. The aryanization of Jewish property had begun. On October 22, 1938, the Nazis announced that they had freed the city of Jews: the last 17 Jewish citizens had just been expelled. Five days later, Rothenburg celebrated the success with a rally. When Kristallnacht struck Germany two weeks later, on November 9, 1938, the Nazi regime had already cleansed the Tauber Valley.

When war broke out, citizens decorated the streets with swastikas, enthusiastically celebrated the victory over Poland, and many felt like innocent victims when an Allied air raid on March 31, 1945 destroyed the town.

▲ The Blasiuskapelle commemorates the fallen of the wars.

Location: Burggarten **Entrance:** Without charge **Opening times:** Always accessible
Internet: http://www.rothenburg-unterm-hakenkreuz.de
Jewish history: https://www.alt-rothenburg.de/juedisches-rothenburg

An Executioner named Rintfleisch

The village Röttingen halfway between Rothenburg and Würzburg was a small town during the Middle Ages that fanatically persecuted all Jews. The reason was *host desecration*. On April 20, 1298, the violent perpetrators marched through town, captured all 21 of the city's Jews and burned them at the stake. Yet, the people were not satisfied. Why? For what reason ... why? The knight Rintfleisch had received a message from heaven. He was meant to become the destroyer of all Jews, and so the butcher moved through Franconia and incited the citizens to pogroms. Many - far too many - followed willingly. The misanthrope was not only successful in Rothenburg. Even in Würzburg and Nürnberg, the citizens submitted to his heavenly vision. More than 5,000 Jews lost their lives during the Rintfleisch Pogrom.

Mittelalterliches Kriminalmuseum

Facts & Figures

The Medieval Crime Museum is one-of-a-kind in Europe. It shows the development of the legal and penal system in southern Germany on four floors. The museum is in the former Johanniter Commandery, built in 1396 for the Order of St John. The exhibition covers the penal system from the Middle Ages to the 19th century. The curators present instruments of torture, shameful punishments and the execution of the death penalty. They use documents to explain the development of the criminal system, present police regulations, illustrate the process of trials and introduce gruesome criminal cases. The museum houses a variety of torture instruments, such as an iron maiden from Nürnberg, neck violins, racks, shame masks, drinking barrels, thumbscrews, spiked chairs, and shame flutes. The exhibits bear witness to a time when violence was used to obtain questionable justice.

During the Middle Ages, the **legal process** and the **execution of a judgment** were cruel spectacles in which the entire population participated. The punishment ranged from pillory to capital punishment. However, as a verdict could only be reached if the defendant was willing to confess, torture was applied in many cases.

An honour punishment was a sentence that resulted in loss of social integration. The punishment at the pillory was only one aspect. The more serious part was the deprivation of civil rights, also known as *Infamia Juris*. The Middle Ages had many ways to implement shameful punishments from the lower courts. For the baker's baptism, the citizens locked a baker in a cage and submerged him under water several times. It was the punishment for rolls that were too small or for stretched flour. Some did not survive the execution.

The authorities punished talkative fellow citizens with a mask of shame. A metal tongue and huge ears symbolised their effervescent personality. The community punished bickering and petty theft with a neck violin: heads and hands were fixed in a wooden chain, and the condemned had to endure ridicule at the pillory. One variant was the

shame flute. It was made of iron and shaped like a flute. Anyone who was condemned to the pillory or the shameful pole was tied to a bar and had to endure not only insults but also beatings. After the violation, the delinquent was cast out of society. Continuing life in the community was often impossible. As a variant, the Middle Ages invented the shame donkey, a bench made of two inclined boards on which the condemned had to sit. The stone of blasphemy was hung on a chain around the neck of those who mocked an honourable citizen unjustly. One may remember! The Middle Ages locked notorious drunkards in a drinking barrel for hours or days.

▲ The citizens submerged the cage under water during a baker's baptism.

Location: Burggasse 3 - 5 **Entrance**: Adults 8,00 €, Concessions 5,00 €
Opening Times: March - October: 10.00 - 18.00, Winter 13:00 - 16:00
Internet: https://www.kriminalmuseum.eu

The Iron Maiden

The execution of any death penalty is horrific, but the Iron Maiden is the culmination of all cruelty. The Mittelalterliche Kriminalmuseum presents a copy of an example from Nürnberg, although experts question its authenticity. The human-sized figure with a female head opened its coat and showed the delinquents its innards: iron spikes. The condemned was forced into the hollow body, and when the executioner closed the iron coat, the bars pierced into his flesh. Death took place immediately; the death struggle was out of sight and hidden. When the kiss of the maiden was completed, as the Nürnberg Chronicle reported in 1533, a trap door opened, and the body fell into the river. A coin forger is said to have died in this way in 1515. However, many historians doubt that the Iron Maiden was ever in use.

St Johannis

Facts & Figures

A chapel was used as a prayer house for the Hospice of the Order of St John during the 13th century. Around 1400, when the city expanded, and the burghers constructed a new wall, the church was torn down, and one in Gothic style was built instead. After the Reformation, the temple

converted to the Protestant faith in 1553. The four-story attic temporarily served as a grain store during the 17th century. After Bavaria had annexed Franconia, the church was returned to the Catholics. The rectangular interior impresses with a crucifix made of silver-plated willowwood: Jesus Christ has broken the shackles and sits on the crossbeam. At the ambo, John the Baptist points out Jesus to his followers, Andrew and John. Both pieces of art are the works of the idiosyncratic Munich artist Klaus Backmund. Tombstones from the 15th century have been preserved along the walls.

The Order of St John in Jerusalem (in German: Johanniter) arrived at the Landwehr in the late 12th century. The monks ran a small hospice in Reichardsroth about ten kilometres north of Rothenburg. Emperor Friedrich I Barbarossa and the nobleman Albrecht von Hohenlohe had donated the property to the order. There, pious knights looked after pilgrims and long-distance traders travelling between Würzburg and Augsburg. Around 1227, the order moved into Rothenburg and opened a hospice at the southern tip of the city. They dedicated the chapel to St John the Baptist. The remains of a tower can be identified on the eastern side of the wall.

As elsewhere, the hospice's peripheral location in Rothenburg was no coincidence. The Inner Council wanted to prevent the transmission of epidemics that pilgrims and other travellers could carry into the city.

The relationship between the magistrate and the Johanniters was not always peaceful. There were many disputes, and not just regarding taxes. Some of them became violent. What is more - anyone who broke out of a prison in Rothenburg asked the Johanniters for church asylum and escaped the enclosure by climbing the wall adjacent to the order.

▲ The Order of St John settled in Rothenburg around 1227.

Heinrich Toppler resolved the conflict by appointing a caretaker of the monastery responsible for overseeing the order's finances and reporting to the Inner Council. The Johanniters had lost the power game. Step by step, the Inner Council controlled their affairs. Over the course of the 15th century, the order lost its popularity and the support of the Rothenburgers. The repeated scuffles had hurt them much.

After the Reformation, the council gave up its restraint and prevented the Order of St John from holding Catholic services. This ultimately marked the end of their community. Finally, the monks left the city during the 16th century.

Location: Burggasse 1 **Entrance:** Without charge
Opening times: Sporadic for prayers and services.
Internet: https://st-johannis-rothenburg.de

A stork for the Storchenapotheke

When the artist Carl Spitzweg visited Rothenburg in June/August 1858, he fell in love with a city still living in the Middle Ages. Carl Spitzweg specialised in depicting the traditional way of life - with a romantic and melancholic touch. He strolled through the city, took sketches with his drawing pen and collected impressions. The painter was a pioneer of Rothenburg's tourism industry. His creativity seduced the romantically inclined middle class to visit the city. And what painted Spitzweg in Rothenburg? A sketchbook kept by the Graphische Staatssammlung München shows his work. The artist later used the impressions as a template for many paintings. The Baumeisterhaus is said to have served as a model for the painting *The Poor Poet*. The painting *Pharmacy with a Stork* was also inspired by his visit to Rothenburg.

Plönlein & Kobolzeller Tor

Facts & Figures

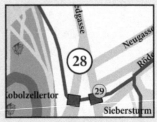

At the picturesque Plönlein between Siebersturm and Kobolzeller Tor, a narrow half-timbered house with a public fountain asks to be photographed. The ensemble is considered Germany's most romantic spot. For the film *Pinocchio* (1940), the producers used the house as a template. In the film *The Wonderful World of the Brothers Grimm*, Karlheinz Böhm posed in front of the fountain. From the Plönlein, a path leads over the Kobolzeller Tor into the Tauber Valley. Charming half-timbered houses line the square on both sides. Their wrought iron signs advertise cafés and restaurants. The Plönlein formerly served as a storage place for fish. The fish trough can be seen on the right. The fountain was built around 1608. It was fed from a spring on the Brühl, which was connected to Rothenburg in 1568. The Plönlein is particularly romantic during evenings.

The saying *"Rothenburg is Plönlein - Plönlein is Rothenburg"* is undoubtedly oversimplified, but it is undeniable that the postcard-worthy motif has become an iconic emblem of Rothenburg. The picturesque spot has defined the city like no other place in Rothenburg. The crooked house next to the well is still inhabited. The basement of the gabled house dates back to the Middle Ages, while the upper floor was added during the 16th century. The facade was renovated in the 19th century. In the past, carpenters, locksmiths and furriers resided in the building.

The triumph of Rothenburg's **tourism industry** began in the mid-19th century thanks to painters like Emil Kirchner, Carl Spitzweg, Toby Rosenthal and others. The artists portrayed an atmosphere that had barely changed since the Thirty Years' War. Their paintings garnered attention both locally and internationally, contributing to the town's popularity as a tourist destination.

When Rothenburg premiered the farce *Der Meistertrunk* at Pentecost in 1881, the officials had discovered tourism as a lucrative source of income. While 50 city dwellers visited the Wildbad above the Tauber River in 1860, in 1900, the city counted 30,000 overnight stays. Today, about 2 million day

▲ The Plönlein is a postcard motif and a flagship of Rothenburg.

tourists visit the city each year. International marketing and word-of-mouth propaganda turned the town into a success story. Japanese, Americans and the English visit the Tauber Valley for an afternoon, make their way through the city and return to their buses. The clichés captivate for a few hours: Imperial City, Middle Ages, charming tranquillity - they promise an escape from our hectic modern life into an ideal world that never existed. The traveller strolls along the Plönlein before visiting the Medieval Crime Museum, which presents the other side of the good old days. Rothenburg thrives on mass tourism. The streets are overcrowded, especially during the summers.

Location: Plönlein **Entrance**: Without charge **Opening times**: Always accessible
Literature: Rothenburg ob der Tauber Daten und Fakten 2019 (Tourismus Service)
Guided tours: http://faszination-rothenburg.de // www.walburga-rothenburg.de

The Kobolzeller Tor

The Kobolzeller Tor secured access to Rothenburg from the Tauber Valley on the city's northern flank - called *Steige*. The citizens built the gate and the inner courtyard as part of the second city wall around 1360. An inner and outer gate fortified the bastion, adorned with the Rothenburg coat of arms and an Imperial Eagle. Any enemy who had overcome the first gate could be shot at from the battlements of the upper level, the so-called Teufelskanzel or devil's pulpit. The adjacent Kohlturm at the southern end provided additional protection. The tower is offset to the side and not located above the entrance because the site was too sloping. A station on Rothenburg's *Way of the Cross* awaited pilgrims at the kennel. Finally, the pious arrived at the Hospice of the Order of St John, where they found shelter for the night.

Facts & Figures

The Johannitertor once protected the southern flank during the 12th century (now demolished). From 1204 onwards, Rothenburg expanded the city by around 200 metres to the south to protect a flourishing area of craftsmen inside the wall. The burghers built today's Siebersturm on Spitalgasse out of sandstone around the year 1385. It separates the old town from the Neue Spital. Here, flour sifters used to go after their trade along the street. The tent-like roof with a lantern at the top was added during the 17th century. In the Middle Ages, the tower was accessed via a ladder on the eastern side. A wooden staircase leads to the entrance today. On the side of the Neue Spital, the defiant humpback blocks surprisingly increase in size. After passing the Siebersturm, one arrives at the neighbourhood Kappenzipfel, which leads towards the Tauber Valley.

Rothenburg also succumbed to **witch hunts**, but hardly anyone was convicted in the city. The Mittelalterliche Kriminalmuseum shows a witch's chair studded with iron nails, on which women had to sit during an embarrassing interrogation. A board of nails stretched over the knees perfected the sadism. The Historiengewölbe shows torture instruments that once were used to support the dreadful truth-finding process.

The persecution of witches peaked in the early modern period, not during the Middle Ages. Between 1550 and 1750, Rothenburg staged 28 trials; 65 people were accused, three women were convicted, and 13 were exiled. In comparison, more than 900 witches lost their lives in Würzburg and around 1,000 women, men and children in Bamberg - in both cities, monasteries ran the Inquisition. The last burning of a witch in Germany occurred in Würzburg in 1749.

Although the Rothenburgers remained level-headed, the city's files refer to witch trials. In 1587, Hans Gackstatter confessed to being in league with the devil. The boy was six years old when he told the judge about a nighttime flight of his mother and a horned man: "They flew over the landscape on a burning iron, stole money, wine and eggs, and they

▲ The Siebersturm was built in 1385 to separate the old town from the Kappenzipfel.

danced in a clearing." The lustre descriptions must have excited the priests. The story led to many rumours within the population, the word went around, and the council had to intervene: the accused were acquitted.

Another case from 1605 tells of the carpenter Hofmann, who must have made a living by earning money through magic. The people accused him of making furniture with the help of spirits who later haunted the wood after the piece was sold. Some claimed that strange noises came from his house - the burghers were very alarmed. The council refrained from using torture and acquitted him, but he probably had to leave the Landwehr.

Location: Plönlein 14 **Entrance:** Without charge **Opening times:** Always accessible
Literature: Hexenprozesse in Rothenburg ob der Tauber (Bachelorarbeit)
Internet: http://www.hexen-franken.de

The Ruckesser and the Faulturm

Before the city expanded to the south, the city wall ran from the tower Ruckesser to the Siebersturm. A part of the wall can still be seen along the alley Sterngasse. The Ruckesser got its name from a Rothenburg family. It means burp or hiccup. In 1813, the city broke a gate for pedestrians through the wall. Until the 18th century, the tower had two additional floors. The monumental 41-metre-tall Faulturm (literally: digestion tower) in the west was used as a prison. The foundations of the building reached four metres deep. Serious criminals were imprisoned there. They were fed through a small hole called Angstloch (fear hole). The robber baron Hans von Craintal supposedly lost his life in the Faulturm in 1426. In 1955, the city discovered the remains of ten human skeletons there, alongside shards dating back to the 15th century.

Facts & Figures

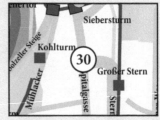

Rothenburg refers to the section between the Siebersturm and the Spitaltor as Kappenzipfel. The Neue Spital, which provided care for the poor and needy, was incorporated into the city wall in 1376. This caused much concern as anyone who studies the morphology of the setting from above will spot immediately: the city wall stretches a long way but only encloses a small strip because it is narrow. This made it difficult to defend the neighbourhood; consequently, the Siebersturm was never torn down to provide additional protection. The motivation for the walling was the hospice's extensive land holdings, by which it influenced the city. The Rossmühle also had to be protected from falling into enemy hands because it supplied Rothenburg with fresh water, which was essential during a siege. The area between the hospice and the old town comprised around 60 houses.

King Albrecht I approved the expansion of Rothenburg in 1298. According to a popular legend, the king compared the blueprint of the enclosure with a sleeping cap. The extension to the south was the tip of the cap, and this is how the name came about: **Kappenzipfel**. The name was not uncommon. Nürnberg, Günzburg, Mindelheim, and Füssen also have suburbs which bear the same name.

The tongue-shaped area was enclosed by the middle of the 14th century. The rapid increase in population during the 13th century made the expansion necessary. The tip of the cap covers a territory of five hectares, and the city wall was extended by 960 metres. The Neue Spital was situated between Rossmühle and Spitaltor in the 13th century; about 60 houses and farms occupied the area between the Order of St John and the Rossmühle. Various craftsmen, whose trade was polluting, had settled there. Among them were blacksmiths and potters. They were joined by cartwrights, who worked almost exclusively in the neighbourhood. Weavers and dyers also moved into the Kappenzipfel. They found drying places in the suburb and could easily descend via the Kobolzeller Steige into the Tauber Valley to the mills.

▲ The romantic Stöberleinsbühne offers enchanting performances under stars.

To the west, the steep slope into the Tauber Valley protected the suburb from attackers. To the east, the wall was fortified by two towers - the Großer Stern (Big Star) and the Kleiner Stern (Little Star) - which were added in the 15th century. The battlement can be walked from the Ruckesser to the Spitaltor. On the side of the field, one can spot the kennel.

The Neue Spital was constructed outside the city wall from 1280 onwards. It was built to complement the Hospice of the Order of St John, which was overcrowded at that time. The city's population was growing, and Rothenburg was a popular stopover for pilgrims travelling along the Jakobswanderweg to Rome.

Location: Spitalgasse **Entrance:** Without charge
Opening times: Always accessible
Internet: http://www.schaefertanzrothenburg.de

Sheep farming at the Neue Spital

The sheep industry was of vital importance in Rothenburg. The Neue Spital's prosperity was also based on sheep farming. The hospice cared for around a thousand sheep that were kept at three locations in the Landwehr: on the Schandtauber, in Schöngras and Arzbach. The herds were taken out to graze in the spring and were looked after by shepherds. A shepherd's wage amounted to one-sixth of the profit earned. During the winter, the animals stayed in barns where the shepherds found accommodation. Counting the herd at the beginning and end of summer determined the revenue for the year. The wool was sheared between late September and early November. It was the basis for the manufacturing of cloth for which Rothenburg was known north of the Alps during the Middle Ages.

(31) Neues Spital

Facts & Figures

The Hospice at the Kappenzipfel was established in 1280 as a Heilig-Geist-Spital (Hospice of the Holy Spirit) for the sick, poor and elderly. It was founded with the help of wealthy burghers from Rothenburg and was called the Neue Spital to distinguish it from the Hospice of the Order of St John. The hospital was located outside the city walls and was therefore accessible to travellers day and night. Donations played a significant role in the growth of the institution, and it soon became the most important commercial enterprise in Rothenburg. The economic power of the Neue Spital was decisive for the hospice being included inside the wall from 1376 onwards. The Hegereiterhaus, built in 1591, stands out with its pointed tent roof and slender stair tower. It is worth seeing. The hospital attendant once lived there, and the kitchen of the hospice was brewing its meals on the ground floor.

The **Neue Spital** (I/III) extended over an area of about 110 to 130 metres, more or less half a kilometre to the south of the Hospice of the Order of St John. It stretched from the Reichsstadthalle to the Spitalgasse and from the Rossmühle to the Spitaltor. The hospice was founded by two canons from Würzburg, Reichsschultheiß Lupoid von Weitingen and Graf Otto von Flügelau. The latter was buried in the hospital church after his death. Many citizens, merchants, and nobles contributed to the construction of the hospice through donations, making the hospital an institution of the *Burgenses et Universitas Populi*, i.e. the citizens and the community as a whole.

A document mentioned the facility for the first time in 1281 (letter of indulgence from Bishop Wichard in Passau), but the concept of the hospice is much older. The nursing home was organised as a double monastery according to the structure of a Holy Spirit Hospital, but it was not subordinate to the Hospitallers. It was based on the rules of the Order of Augustinians. Nuns and brothers worked at the double monastery side by side to provide care - management had to keep a keen eye on the moral conduct of the community.

The hospital provided essential services to the sick and poor. Beneficiaries could buy into the community to provide for their retirement. Pilgrims were also welcome at the hospice. They paid with prayers for the salvation of the founders' souls. The Holy Blood Pilgrimage began in the late 13th century. It is believed that the hospital was established to accommodate the increasing number of pilgrims.

The Neue Spital was built outside the city walls. Like other cities, Rothenburg wanted to avoid infectious diseases, and separation was the only measure to protect the local population from illnesses for which there was no cure, like leprosy or the black death.

▲ A document mentions the Neue Spital in 1281 for the first time.

Location: Spitalgasse **Entrance:** Without charge **Opening times:** Always accessible
Spitalkirche: Opening times: sunrise to sunset.
Internet: http://rothenburg-evangelisch.de/unsere-kirchen/heilig-geist-kirche-oder-spitalkirche

The Spitalkirche

At Spitalgasse 46, the church of the hospital guarded the spiritual life of the residents. The Rothenburgers laid the founding stone for the Gothic church in 1281 and added the slender tower in 1308. The building was extensively restored in 1591. The main altar of the narrow, single-nave church is decorated with a crucifix and the figures of Mary and John. They were carved in 1430. The stone sculpture of the Virgin Mary on the right side was created around 1330. The sacrament house shows the Annunciation of Mary (around 1390). Tombs refer to patrons and donors. Among them, the gravestone of Graf Otto von Flügelau, who died in 1317, stands out. It is next to the altar. Interestingly, the priests celebrated mass there according to reformed liturgy as early as 1542, some six years before the conversion of Rothenburg to Protestantism.

(32) Rossmühle

Facts & Figures

Rothenburg relied on local springs and the Tauber River for its water. The Bronnenmühle, located in the valley, used to pump drinking water to the Klingentor, from where it was distributed throughout the city. However, during a siege, the pumping station could fall into enemy

hands, and therefore, the council decided to build one within the city walls. The burghers constructed the Rossmühle around 1516. Up to 16 horses powered four pumping stations. The equipment could also grind grain. Today, the old building is home to one of Germany's most beautiful youth hostel, a must-stay for anyone travelling the region. Another curiosity: a small opening has been preserved in the wall of the battlement at the height of the Rossmühle, which once served as a toilet. The building opposite was used to farm sheep. It was the second-largest barn in the city and was built between 1500 and 1550.

The **Neue Spital** (II/III) was self-sufficient and under self-management when it was founded. The complex provided accommodation for the poor, sick, and for pilgrims, it held services at its church, and it organised farmsteads. The number of buildings was so large that the complex was considered a city within a city. Until the end of the 14th century, it operated without much pressure from the magistrate.

The so-called Alte Pfründe were located in today's courtyard north of the hospital church. The three-story hospital also had a section for the mentally ill. The premises were demolished in 1823. The main building next to today's Stöberleinsbühne housed the hospital administration until the 16th century. Next to it was the plague house. Today's Reichsstadthalle served as a tithe barn.

The hospital attendant lived on the upper floor of the Hegereiterhaus in the middle of the complex. The hospital kitchen was located on its ground floor. The hospice had bakeries, a bathhouse, and a dairy. A house for the clergy and a small library with a writing room completed the ensemble.

A detailed set of rules described what kind of help any client could

▲ Today, the former Rossmühle houses Germany's most stunning youth hostel.

receive. This also applied to those benefactors who had bought their way into the hospital. They lived in a separate house and enjoyed modest luxury depending on their invested interest.

After the Order of St John had left the city, the entire social welfare system was under the control of the Neue Spital. Those who could not support themselves could receive help from the hospice - mostly, however, pastoral encouragement.

Politically, the institution was of enormous importance: it appeased the worst class differences and thus prevented revolts from breaking out in an oligarchic urban society where only few had a say.

Youth Hostel Rossmühle: Mühlacker 1, Bed & Breakfast 28,40 €
https://www.jugendherberge.de/jugendherbergen/rothenburg-ob-der-tauber-263
Stöberleinsbühne: http://www.stoeberleinsbuehne.de

The Stöberleinsbühne

A city initiative to support young unemployed professionals built an open-air theatre with 165 seats directly next to the Stöberleinsturm in the Spitalviertel. Its performances staged under a starry sky are most atmospheric. The citizens' project was handed over to the magistrate on May 30, 2008. Joyful festivities accompanied the act. So far, the amphitheatre has hosted Irish folk music, dance events, jazz concerts, tango shows and classical music. With the support of the city and numerous Rothenburger businesses, some unemployed achieved a qualification with the project and secured, therefore, further employment later. The stage is available for rent from the Kulturforum für Veranstaltungen (cultural office of Rothenburg). An alternative stage is also accessible in case of bad weather.

(33) Reichsstadthalle

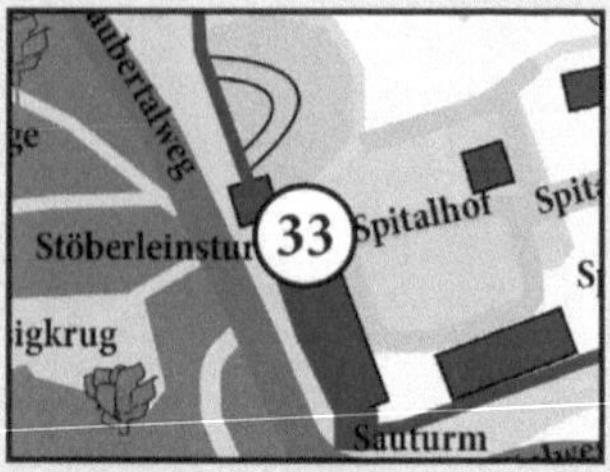

Facts & Figures

At the southwest end of the hospital, parallel to the city wall, the Reichsstadthalle is an event venue that seats up to 550 people. The hospital's former tithe barn was built in 1699 and, after being redesigned, was integrated into Rothenburg's cultural program as an event location in the year 1975. Here, the hospital kept the tax levy on their farms, which had to be paid not in money but in kind. Today, the historical rooms are used as a modern conference space. The solid wooden ceiling, stone walls and parquet floor offer a rural backdrop for concerts, theatre and cabaret performances. The architecturally appealing hall impresses with its sophisticated lighting system. The Reichsstadthalle can be rented for private events from Rothenburg's Zentrale Immobilienmanagement, the city's real estate management. Catering is, of course, included.

The **Neue Spital** (III/III) was organised similarly to a monastic order. Obedience and chastity were virtues that equally applied to the retired and patients. Donations were the foundation of its operations, making it the most prosperous institution in the city. Emperor Ludwig der Bayer granted a letter of protection in 1330, thereby ensuring the integrity of the charity. The hospital depended on craftsmen, cooks, maids and other support to keep its facilities running. However, nuns and brothers were the residents' primary caregivers.

The hospital was a crucial economic factor in the Imperial City. It had scattered land holdings, but the hospice succeeded in moving most of its economic area through land exchange inside the Landwehr. It had considerable land holdings. Principals overlooked the farms. The hospice grew grain, kept sheep and cultivated vineyards. In good years, the hospital sold up to 300 sheep to butchers in Nürnberg. With three farms, the institution became the city's largest landholder during the 16th century.

The economic strength of the hospital motivated the Inner Council to take charge of its administration. Gradually, the patricians replaced the fraternal organisation with a hierarchical structure and infiltrated a

▲ In the former tithe barn, a conference centre welcomes course participants.

council member to oversee the organisation. From the 14th century onwards, the magistrate appointed loyal vicars and nominated two hospital nurses from their ranks. With the help of administrators, they took control of the facility. By then, the monastic organisation was so weakened that the fraternity could not push back. From the late 15th century onwards, the hospital master was almost always recruited from one of the patrician families. Step by step, the city took control of the hospice, and the oligarchic regime ousted anyone from power who was not part of their circle. The hierarchical structure was God-given, and the patricians made sure it was.

Reichsstadthalle: Spitalhof 8 **Opening Times:** Only for events
Zentrales Immobilienmanagement: Grüner Markt 1, 91541 Rothenburg ob der Tauber
Tel: 09861 / 404-462 E-Mail: nadja.bruder@rothenburg.de

The Stöberleinsturm

The Stöberleinsturm protects the Kappenzipfel at the so-called Sausteige (steep path of the swine), directly at the northern end of the Reichsstadthalle. A wooden staircase leads to the battlement that can be walked. It is the only tower that still has an original finish: a tent roof with four hexagonal bay windows. Two angels carry the Imperial Eagle on the outside. They are supported by a third angel who spreads his wings over two city coats of arms. The tower was built around 1376. During the 17th century, the structure served the city as a mental asylum. According to legend, Mayor Stöberlein was imprisoned here for treason during the urban war. The tower is also called the Hundsturm (tower of the dogs), as voracious dogs were kept here. They were trained to guard the city moat.

Facts & Figures

The Spitaltor (gate to the hospice) secured the Kappenzipfel to the south. Work on the tower began around 1370. After it was destroyed in 1631, Rothenburg rebuilt the tower. The gate was reinforced with a moat and a drawbridge, which can still be seen today. The city coat of arms and an Imperial

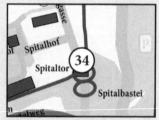

Eagle adorn the outer wall. A trap gate prevented access on the city side. Its grooves survived. The burghers added the two bastions to the front of the gate between 1580 and 1586. They form the structure of an 8. The fortification was the answer to the invention of firearms. The complex included seven gates, six towers and a massive, five-story principal tower. The path through the barbican curves twice, making it difficult for attackers to breach the entry with a battering ram. The Spitaltor has the motto: *"Peace to those who enter. Hail to the one who leaves."* (Friede den Eintretenden. Heil den Hinausgehenden.)

Water was a precious commodity in medieval Rothenburg. The first **bathers** began their work in the 14th century. By the time the modern era had arrived, there were five bathing facilities in town. The Bürgerbad and the Pfäffleinsbad were two of the popular ones. A barber had to complete several years of training and, after an examination by the city physicist, was responsible for a large variety of services, from hair cutting to minor surgical procedures.

The running of a bathhouse was under the supervision of the Inner Council. Bathing regulations defined the process. Hygiene was the top priority. Bathers performed bloodlettings and extracted teeth, which was life-threatening for patients because of risk of infection. During wartime, bathers were also permitted to perform amputations. However, an injured's chance of survival was slim: infection and painful shock killed many of the wounded.

The council founded a pharmacy on the Marktplatz in the early 14th century. From 1374 onwards, the **pharmacist** was an employee of the city. He had to complete an apprenticeship and swear an oath upon starting his profession.

▲ The Spitaltor protected the Kappenzipfel with an extensive barbican.

Medical doctors specialised in internal diseases. They carried out major surgeries and monitored the healthcare system. Documents mention Rothenburg's first medic in 1303 - a Jew. Two professionals from Rothenburg even rose to become honourable professors in Tübingen during their careers.

Midwives helped women to deliver babies. Childbirth was their speciality. During the Middle Ages, the birth of a child was a dangerous affair for the mother, and the Inner Council kept a close eye on the midwives. Since no female medics were allowed at that time, their experience was always highly appreciated among women.

Location: Spitalgasse 55 **Entrance:** Without charge **Opening Times:** Always accessible **Playgrounds:** https://www.rothenburg.de/stadtplan/stadtplan-kinderspielplaetze **City magazine:** http://www.rotour.de

Children's playgrounds

Rothenburg is a playground for children, not only because the medieval city wall with its battlements and towers is most adventurous but because adventure playgrounds encourage to be jolly. A playground is located directly at the Ruckesser, where the second city wall leads into the one of the Kappenzipfel. Another playground can be found on Hornburgweg. The most exciting ensemble, however, is located on the Klosterweth next to the Strafturm (penalty tower). Of course, they all provide a sandpit, a slide, swings and a seesaw, but there, the attraction is a climbing wall and an extensive playhouse. And everything is framed by wildflowers and limestone. Rothenburg's playgrounds are an enchanting experience for young and old and an alternative for families with young children to spend an hour or two while having a picnic.

Facts & Figures

At Taubertalweg 42 below the Spital-bastei, the orthopedist Friedrich Hessing from Göggingen commissioned a monumental spa hotel in historicist style in 1894 (opened in 1902). At some point after the earthquake of 1356, shepherds discovered a spring with sulphurous water.

Back then, the citizens were bathing in the fountain of youth at the slope leading to the Tauber Valley. The spa ceased to operate during World War I. When the Nazi regime took over, the complex served as a training centre for the Hitler Youth. After World War II, the Protestant Church acquired the building in 1978 and converted it into a conference centre. Over 50 guest rooms on three floors are available. The Wildbad is committed to culture. It organises art exhibitions, classical music events and the electronic music festival Sundowner. The handsome garden is open to anyone interested.

The Tauber Valley ran on mills. Between Wildbad and Detwang, twelve mills once grounded grain; they served as sawmills or pumped water up the cliff to Rothenburg. The mills gave Rothenburg its prosperity and allowed the city to survive. However, they are located outside the city walls. Their loss during a siege was life-threatening. The Förderverein Taubermühlenweg e. V. (a nonprofit organisation) has made it its mission to preserve the mills, research their history and educate the public. Their interesting **Taubermühlenweg** (hiking path from mill to mill) brings the past to life.

The busy Schwabenmühle was below today's Evangelische Tagungsstätte (Protestant conference centre). A document mentioned it in 1340 for the first time. It used to grind grain with the power of water. An additional sawmill cut wood. Friedrich Hessing, the founder of the spa hotel Wildbad, converted the mill into a model farmstead during the 19th century. He wanted to offer his guests fresh fruits and vegetables: "*Straight from the tree, fresh onto the plate.*" was his slogan. Over the years, he added farm buildings and stables.

The Fuchsmühle, first mentioned in 1447, was operational until 1989.

It was the last producing mill in the region. Currently, it is a residential building, but the wheels turned again in 2010 to generate electricity.

The Bronnenmühle at the hiking path Kurzer Steig used a lifting mechanism to pump water from the Tauber River into a reservoir at the Klingentor. The complex was equipped with a grain mill and a sawmill. The Kempten designer Hans Sommer & Son built the "Rothenburger Neue Wasserkunst" in 1593, a pumping station that pumped water from the Tauber River 80 metres up via four cylinders. The pipe was 350 metres long and hidden from enemy eyes. The city stopped its operations in 1950.

▲ The Evangelische Tagungsstätte hosts seminars and conferences.

Evangelische Tagungsstätte: Taubertalweg 42, 91541 Rothenburg o.d.T.
Internet: https://wildbad.de **Garden:** *Rothenburger Gartenparadiese* (Tourismus Service)
Taubermühlenweg: https://www.taubermuehlenweg.de

Melusine, the beautiful

The miller at the Eulschirbenmühle north of Tauberbischofsheim had a maid who was not only beautiful but also hardworking. Her name was Melusine. On Thursday evenings, however, she would sneak out, run along the stream to a hidden clearing, undress and turn into a graceful water maiden. One day, Graf von Gamburg saw her, followed her, and discovered her secret. Overcome with love, he stole her clothes after she had jumped into the water. The mermaid had no choice but to become the count's lover. The nobleman built a hidden castle at the Tauber River, where the two enjoyed their romance with lute music and dancing. This soon aroused the miller's curiosity until he discovered their secret. The lamentation was great: the nymph dissolved, and the count fell ill. He died a few months later of a broken heart.

Facts & Figures

The Tauber River has its source in Wettringen, twenty kilometres south of Rothenburg. It flows into the river Main near the city of Wertheim to the west of Würzburg. From source to mouth, the stream spans about 130 kilometres and covers an altitude of nearly 300 metres. The Tauber River is Rothenburg's lifeline. In the past, it supplied the city with drinking water and powered mills. Now, it is a local recreation area. The Tauber River has been an engine of prosperity since the Middle Ages. It is the namesake of Tauberfranken and the Tauber Valley. The name *Tauber* is believed to have originated from the Celtic word *Dubron*, meaning fast-flowing water. The Burggasse and the Burggarten above the river offer the best vantage points to enjoy the serene Tauber Valley. From there, one gets a good overview of the region's geography and agricultural use.

During the Ice Age, tectonic uplifts formed the **Tauber Valley**. Exogenous processes such as heavy rainfall subsequently led to extensive soil erosion. Below the Schandtauber (a tributary), the river dug into the shell limestone, creating a serpentine meandering.

The mixed forest along the Tauber River is a sight to behold. One finds deciduous trees such as limes, beeches and oaks. Feather grass, whitebeams and orchids grow in their shade. The flora is adapted to draughts during summers and attracts sand lizards, stag beetles and butterflies. Even frogs and salamanders can be discovered alongside bats. Wild boars, foxes, hares and badgers roam the forests. In addition, storks, owls, buzzards and hawks glide through the air; dippers and kingfishers breed along the shores of the Tauber River.

Grapevines grow on the slopes of the Tauber Valley to this day. Vintners press them into traditional brands. In addition to the Tauberschwarz, the Silvaner, Dornfelder, Schwarzriesling and Müller-Thurgau are harvested. Some winemakers offer tours around their vineyards, including a sample of their products at the end.

Orchards join the vines with apple and pear trees. Beekeepers also enjoy

▲ The Tauber River is a stream, 130 kilometres long, flowing into the Main.

a rich harvest in the Tauber Valley. During the Middle Ages, fishermen made good catches and sold their capture to the burghers at the Plönlein, keeping them fresh in troughs.

The water of the Tauber River has powered mills since the Middle Ages. Their remains can be spotted along the winding path following the stream. A beer garden at the Bronnenmühle provides access to the river in the shade of chestnut trees.

Attempts to make the Tauber River navigable failed due to the cost of the locks that would have had to be built. Today, small hydroelectric power plants use the river to generate electricity. They contribute to protecting the climate.

Landscape and vintners: https://www.liebliches-taubertal.de
Taubertal-Festival (August): https://taubertal-festival.de
see also: https://www.frankentourismus.de/orte/rothenburg_odt-387

The Taubertal-Festival at the Eiswiese

Once a year, on the second weekend in August, the Eiswiese (ice meadow) opposite the Bronnenmühle welcomes around 20,000 music fanatics to a rock and pop festival lasting several days. In the shadow of the enchanting old town, nationally and internationally known artists perform on two stages. Many stars line up to get the show going. The Fantastische Vier, Placebo, Antilopen Gang, Feine Creme Fischfilet, Kraftclub and the Beatsteaks were among them. Irish groups such as Fiddler's Green and Flogging Molly also regularly participate in the event. Thanks to the exhilarating audience, the atmosphere is at a boiling point. Pounding beats burn the experience into the synapses of the brain forever. One should bring a small tent and sleeping bags, leave all valuables at home and look forward to three days of exuberant frolic!

(37) Doppelbrücke

Facts & Figures

The Tauber River is a picturesque stream that babbles romantically most of the time and rarely bursts over its banks (warning: flood of 1732). So! Why the monumental Doppelbrücke (double bridge) that stretches over the waters below the Kalkturm? One wonders!- The transition resembles a Roman viaduct with seven arches of different widths at the bottom and ten equivalent arches at the top. The bridge was built around 1330. A defensive tower secured the Kobolzeller Steige, leading to the Kobolzeller Tor. To get to Rothenburg, carts needed additional horses to overcome the incline. The wagoners must have earned good money, as the long-distance route from Frankfurt to Nürnberg passed over the bridge. On April 16, 1945, the Wehrmacht blew up the crossing - a futile attempt to delay the advancement of the Allied troops.

On April 16, 1945, the day the Wehrmacht blew up the Doppelbrücke over the Tauber River (the Nazis had set up a fighting post at the Wildbad), six US soldiers with a white flag made their way to Rothenburg and demanded the city to **surrender** without a fight. "They called us bastards!" recalls one of the nervous negotiators. "And we only wanted to save the goddamn city from further destruction." Along the way, they were spat on by Rothenburgers – by Rothenburgers who had voted 83% for Adolf Hitler back in 1933.

At about 6 a.m. the following day, the 1st American Battalion of the 12th Regiment moved into the city, supported by the 4th Infantry Division. The Marktplatz was deserted. The SS, the Volkssturm and the Wehrmacht had hastily fled towards the Frankenhöhe. Just days before, Rothenburg's district leader had issued a different order: "The city will be defended to the last man." Tank traps and ambushes were hastily set up to stop the advancement of the American troops. Those Rothenburgers who advocated abandoning the city were insulted, and they were threatened with retaliation. The mood was tense.

On April 10, the Wehrmacht withdrew from the city. According to

▲ The Doppelbrücke over the Tauber River points the way to Nürnberg.

eyewitnesses, the German soldiers had "physically and mentally collapsed". Finally, a new order arrived from the headquarters: "The Rothenburg combat section must be evacuated on the night of April 16th to 17th." Within a few hours, all soldiers fled, and the Wildbad fighting position was abandoned.

On the afternoon of April 17, the remaining policemen put down their arms and changed into civilian clothes. Citizens handed over their weapons at the police station. The Americans set up military posts on Herrngasse, and confiscated a hotel, which was converted into an army hospital. Within a few hours, a new era had begun.

Doppelbrücke: https://www.brueckenweb.de
Nazi regime in Rothenburg: http://www.rothenburg-unterm-hakenkreuz.de
Leyk's Lotos Garten: https://www.lotos-garten.de

Leyk's Lotos Garden

At Erlbacher Straße 108, entrepreneur Bernd Schulz-Leyk fulfilled a long-cherished dream: an Asian lotus garden. A 250-year-old, richly ornamented gate from India welcomes visitors to the 3,000 square metre garden hidden behind a high wall. Almost a third of the complex is covered by ponds fed by babbling waterfalls and gentle streams. A red bridge leads over the water, showing the way to enlightenment on the other side. A tea house invites its guests to meditate and relax. Exotic plants, a dragon hole and pagodas tempt anyone to respite from the sorrows of everyday life. Japanese dwarf juniper, bamboo, arborvitae, cherry trees, and irises entice the soul to wander about and contemplate. The idea of the garden is to leave the noise of modernity behind - just for a moment.

(38) Kobolzeller Kapelle

Facts & Figures

The former late Gothic Marian pilgrimage church was erected in 1472 on a hermitage established during the 12th century. According to dendrochronological studies, the rampart roof was constructed in 1496. The chapel was a prayer house for pilgrims. A double spiral staircase (one up, one down) ensured a smooth visit. The structure indicates that the chapel must have been very popular at the turn of the 16th century. During the Peasants' Revolt in 1525, the millers of Rothenburg looted the church. They had been incited by the theologian Andreas Karlstadt: The mob smashed statues, tore up pictures and threw the shards into the Tauber River. A tannery used the empty building as a barn until King Maximilian II restored the church in 1853. The single-nave church was reconsecrated in 1860. Today, a lovely Madonna adorns the altar. It dates from the 15th century and was carved in Nürnberg.

Rothenburg is situated along the **Romantische Straße** (Romantic Road), which stretches from Augsburg, Nördlingen, Dinkelsbühl and Tauberbischofsheim to Füssen and Würzburg. The city above the Tauber River is undoubtedly the highlight of this romantic route, but other towns also offer delightful vineyards, half-timbered houses, turrets and battlements. The highway of German romanticism was initiated in 1950 to draw attention to Germany as a holiday destination and thus keep the German Mark within Germany. During the COVID-19 pandemic, many cyclists rediscovered the 500-kilometre-long route. Their path is sensibly signposted to avoid most of the busy roads.

Rothenburg also lies along the **Burgenstraße** (Castle Road), which runs from Mannheim via Heidelberg to Nürnberg and Bayreuth. It is one of Europe's oldest long-distance travel roads and impresses with a shining history. Over 770 kilometres, the route passes 60 castles and palaces. Highlights include Heidelberg Castle, Schwetzingen Castle, the Imperial Castle in Nürnberg, and the Wagner House in Bayreuth.

Rothenburg is tightly interwoven with its surrounding area and serves as a gateway to other attractions in the region. It is a highlight in southern

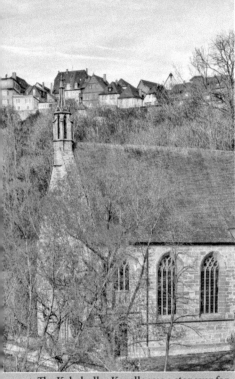

▲ The Kobolzeller Kapelle was a stopover for pilgrims on their way to Rome.

Germany - certainly - but it is only one attraction amongst many.

In Schillingsfürst, visitors are welcomed by the baroque castle of a nobleman. In Bad Windsheim, travellers await an open-air museum and an exciting thermal spa. The village Feuchtwangen boasts a local history museum, and Dinkelsbühl has preserved its city fortifications. In Ansbach, a lovely orangery enchants visitors, and Bad Mergentheim offers a relaxing Solymar thermal spa.

And Würzburg? Würzburg teems with saints, apostles and angels who fly low through the city and whoosh over the vineyards. They dig into souls and burn witches.

Kobolzeller Kapelle: Schloßstr. 17 **Opening Times**: Only during services.
Internet: https://st-johannis-rothenburg.de/kirchen/kobolzell-unsere-liebe-frau
Travel Routes: https://www.romantischestrasse.de // https://www.burgenstrasse.de

The Rothenburg Leprosyium

With the Crusades in the 13th century, a new disease swapped over Europe: leprosy. Rothenburg had to protect its burghers and built a leprosarium about two kilometres south of the Spitaltor on the Gebsattel. The infirmary was dedicated to Saint Leonhard. It was first mentioned in 1305. A new building was constructed around 1348. The sick were permitted to beg in the streets as long as they could be identified as lepers and approached their target against the wind. In 1549, the leprosy was a part of the Neue Spital. Since 1550, a committee of medical doctors, surgeons, and pharmacists have made the diagnosis of who had to be admitted. After the disease subsided in Europe during the 18th century, the house served as an educational institution for orphaned children from 1867 onwards.

Facts & Figures

Around 1388, the mayor of Rothenburg, Heinrich Toppler, built a small castle on the Taubertalweg. Rothenburg's coat of arms adorned the privately owned property. It is open to visits by appointment only. Inside, wooden furniture and accessories from the region show the bourgeois lifestyle from the 16th to 19th centuries. The living space some metres above resembles the family tower of a nobleman. Heinrich Toppler enjoyed the manor as a summer residence where he discussed the future of the Landwehr with noblemen. Even King Wenzel was a guest. The Rothenburgers believed that Toppler wanted to keep an eye on the Taubermühlen, which is why he built the castle. They nicknamed him the *King of Rothenburg*. The satire of power escalated to his violent death in 1408: An oligarchic regime cannot accept a primus inter pares for long if the patricians want to keep their privileges.

The patrician **Heinrich Toppler** lived with his family close to the Marktplatz at Obere Schmiedgasse 5. He served as the mayor of Rothenburg for most of the years between 1373 and 1408. During his tenure, the city reached the culmination of its power, with the Inner Council expanding its control to 350 square kilometres. The Landwehr stretched from Steinach in the east to Wettringen in the west. From 1430 onwards, the Landhege (a rural moat) defended the area. Guarded towers overlooked all arterial roads. Parts of the fortifications have been preserved, such as the tower near Lichtel. At that time, almost 170 settlements are recorded in the area.

Heinrich Toppler was born in the 1340s as the son of a wealthy cattle farmer. His father was a patrician and a member of the Inner Council. At the age of 23, he was promoted to mayor. Already back then, Heinrich Toppler was willing to take risks. For example, he strengthened the city's standing by purchasing land from members of the impoverished rural nobility. He quickly became the wealthiest citizen in Rothenburg, but other patricians also enriched themselves.

From 1375 onwards, Jews settled again in Rothenburg, and, as

donors, they financed the city's growth with loans. When Heinrich Toppler built the Topplerschlösschen around 1388, he certainly felt like a member of the nobility. At that time, his power grew as quickly as the number of those who were envious.

In 1376, his friendship with Wenzel of Luxembourg bore fruit: the son of Emperor Karl IV was crowned king that year. Heinrich Toppler's political influence reached as far as the Reichstag. Then, he overplayed his cards and lost a military conflict against Nürnberg and its ally, the Bishop of Würzburg. Heinrich Toppler died in the dungeon of the Rothenburg town hall in 1408.

▲ Mayor Heinrich Toppler built the manor in the Tauber Valley around 1388.

Topplerschlösschen: Taubertalweg 100
Opening Times: Only by prior appointment. Miss Boas telephone: 09861 / 7358
Internet: http://www.heinrich-toppler.de

A cycle path called Liebliches Taubertal

Franconia is a paradise for cyclists. Numerous routes run through the landscape. From Rothenburg, a cycle path leads across the Tauber Valley from Weikersheim and Tauberbischofsheim to Wertheim am Main. The route spans a distance of one hundred kilometres. Anyone who starts in Rothenburg will enjoy that the tour leads mostly downhill towards the northwest, but headwinds can challenge the peddlers. The ADFC awarded the route five stars - the best qualification possible. Along the way, the cyclists pass numerous sights, including eleven palaces, eight fortresses, six monasteries and 46 museums. The Nature Park Frankenhöhe motivates the effort even when it rains with charming vineyards and wild nature. The tour takes about three days, depending on sporting ambition and cultural interest.

St Peter und Paul in Detwang

Facts & Figures

Documents mention Detwang in 960 for the first time. The idyllic village is northwest of Rothenburg and adjacent to the Tauber River. The farmstead is thus at least one hundred years older than the castle at the Kappenzipfel and at least two hundred years older than Rothenburg.

In the 10th century, the farmers consecrated the Romanesque parish church of St Peter und Paul. It is the oldest fortified chapel in Franconia, saving the souls of many Rothenburgers. By 1258, it was in the hands of the Deutscher Ritterorden. Tilman Riemenschneider carved the church's Heilig-Kreuz-Altar (Holy Cross altar) in lime wood around 1508. The masterpiece was initially intended for the Michaelskapelle in Rothenburg but was moved to Detwang in 1653. The side altars show saints and the Virgin Mary with Child. The figures were created between 1480 and 1510.

The **Heilig-Kreuz-Altar** (Holy Cross altar) in the Church of St Peter und Paul Detwang by the artist Tilman Riemenschneider is the highlight of any tour along the Tauber Valley. The carver was born in Thüringen in 1460 and died in Würzburg in 1531. Experts admire his works for their delicate technique, which he perfected when the Renaissance was about to take over from the late Gothic. Archetypal representations are increasingly being replaced by lifelike figures that reveal the character and emotionality of the people depicted. The artist created the Heilig-Blut-Altar for the Church of St Jakob by 1505. Its brother, the Heilig-Kreuz-Altar in Detwang, was carved around 1508 for the Michaelskapelle, which accompanied the souls of the dead into eternity next to the cemetery.

The altar shows Jesus in the middle. His head dropped wearily onto his right shoulder; his mouth is slightly open, and his feet are crossed. Death has occurred: the wound of the lance below the ribs on his right side is an unmistakable sign. The naturalistic depiction shows Christ as a suffering man who, emaciated, consumes himself in pain.

On the left, a group of three women mourns the death of Jesus. They are joined by the Virgin Mary and the evangelist John. Tears well up

▲ The chapel in Detwang is one of the oldest fortified churches in Franconia.

in her eyes; she crosses her arms. On the right, Pharisees and mercenaries observe the death of the Messiah. Their uniforms are medieval, their faces are stern. Scrutinizing scepticism is written all over their foreheads.

The stunning relief on the left wing shows Jesus preying on the Mount of Olives. His hands are folded in front of his chest. In despair, he looks to the sky; his disciples sleep at his feet. They cover their left eyes; their faces are full of deep furrows.

The right-wing relief is dedicated to the Resurrection of the Saviour. He has overcome death and raises two fingers in glory to bless the world.

Location: Detwang 30 **Entrance:** Adults 1,50 €, Concessions 1,00 €
Opening Times: April - October Mon - Sat 10.00 - 12.00 / Sun 14.00 - 16.00
Internet: http://rothenburg-evangelisch.de/unsere-kirchen/st-peter-und-pauls-kirche-detwang

The Devil's Stone from Detwang

The devil was furious - outraged: The pious Franks had built yet another house of worship, this time in Detwang. He ordered one of his assistants to destroy the temple with a large stone just before its consecration, but en route, the apprentice lost his way. When he asked an elderly mother for directions, she sensed danger. "I have worn out my shoes", she told him, "since I have left the chapel." To prove her claim, she showed him the soles in her basket, which all had holes. "I got through them all!" she grumbled. "The way is long." The devilish journeyman lost all hope, threw the heavy stone off his back and left. The crone was the wife of a shoemaker. Her clever wit has saved the nearby church in Detwang from the works of Satan, and, only therefore, it still stands unharmed today for us to visit.

(41) Rothenburg-View

The **agricultural industry** has always dominated the Rothenburger Landwehr. Until the turn of the century, some farmers lived inside the city wall. Today, almost a quarter of the population earns their living from farming, many from livestock. The upstream and downstream industries, such as seed manufacturers or dairies, double the percentage. Nationwide, around 13% of Bavaria's population is directly or indirectly employed in agriculture. At the turn of the millennium, on average, a farmer owned around 30 hectares of land.

During the Middle Ages, most people in the Landwehr exclusively worked in the agricultural sector. Apart from millers, hardly any craftsmen settled outside of Rothenburg. Generally, the villages were too small to allow for a division of labour. A full farmer cultivated about ten acres of land. Compared to today, his crop yield was ten times lower. Epidemics, hail and storms, and plundering troops resulted in severe hunger. A half-farmer tilled half that area, a quarter-farmer managed less than three acres, and a Köbler couldn't fill his stomach even in good years. Each village was in service to the city, had to pay levies to the Inner Council, and the people had to obey the laws passed by the patricians.

Farmers were an everyday presence in Rothenburg. They delivered goods to the market, served the patricians, constructed the city wall and other public buildings, and maintained the infrastructure. In return, they acquired essential everyday items from the craftsmen in the city - but only those they could not produce themselves.

During the 14th century, the lower rural nobility became impoverished. It was the era of Heinrich Toppler, who rose to become a large landowner. At this time, many knights became dependent on a regional Lord through no fault of their own. The alternative was to become a farmer without a future, and many loathed this fate.

▲ This is how the engraver Matthäus Merian the Elder saw Rothenburg in 1648.

Ski Jump Rothenburg: Leuzenbronner Straße, 850 m after the Doppelbrücke
Kletterwald Rothenburg: Blinksteige, Opening Times: bookings only online
Entrance: Adults 20.00 €, Concessions 13.00 €, Internet: https://kletterwald-rothenburg.com

The Kletterwald Rothenburg

An ultimate thrill awaits adventurers at the Amerikanerwäldchen just after the Dopplelbrücke. Where the Landwehr presents the best view of Rothenburg, a small entertainment park invites the daring to climb trees. The motto is: "*Up the tree.*" The organisers installed 140 climbing elements along 14 courses that test courage and skill. Like Tarzan, one swings from tree to tree on lianas, balances over floating bridges, and whizzes along ropes 120 metres through the forest with a climbing harness. The challenges are up to 17 metres tall, but the courses suitable for the whole family offer an adrenaline cocktail, too. If one prefers to go high, one may book a ride with *Happy Ballooning* to take a trip with a balloon over the Tauber Valley and experience Rothenburg from a birds-eye view.

Index

A

ADFC 14, 119
Aischgrund 21
Allied air raid 8, 13, 17, 53, 63, 66, 67, 69, 74, 91
Alte Gymnasium 1, 53
Alte Pfründe 104
Alter Stadtgraben 68, 69
Altmühlterme 15
Alt-Rothenburger Handwerkerhaus 3, 17, 25, 68, 69
Amerikanerwäldchen 14, 123
Amsterdam 38, 82
Ansbach 36, 117
Arbeitsgemeinschaft für jüdische Geschichte 13, 89
Arzbach 101
Athis Mons 88
Augsburg 1, 36, 94, 116

B

Backmund, Klaus 18, 94
Baden-Wuerttemberg 74
Bad Mergentheim 117
Bad Windsheim 15, 117
Balloon rides 14, 123
Bamberg 98
bathers 108
battlements 62
Battle of Lipan 71
Battle of Nördlingen 12, 67
Baumeisterhaus 43, 56, 95
Bavaria 8, 49, 70, 71, 74, 75, 77, 94
Bayerisches Denkmalamt 9, 67
Bayreuth 70, 116
Bergoglio, Jorge Mario 13, 85
Berlichingen, Dietrich von 84
Berlichingen, Götz von 84
Bezoldweg 25
Biscoph, Samuel 72
Bishop Wichard 102
Blasiuskapelle 6, 17, 26, 88, 90, 91
Böhm, Karlheinz 96
Brettheim 49
Bronnenmühle 29, 58, 104, 111, 113

Bruderschaft der Schäfer 12, 25, 45
Brühl 66, 96
Buenos Aires 85
Burgeck 86
Burgenstraße 2, 116
Bürgerbad 108
Burggarten 5, 10, 13, 17, 26, 29, 36, 86, 88, 89, 91, 112
Burggasse 93, 95, 112
Burgtor 86, 87
Büttelhaus 71

C

Catholic League 2, 7, 12, 24, 36, 39, 40, 60, 62, 64
Chicago World's Fair 8
Children's Playgrounds 14, 109
Christian, Kaspar 84
City Archive 71
Coalition War 74
Coemeterium Judaeorum 77
Council of Constance 70
COVID-19 pandemic 9, 116
Craintal, Hans von 99
Crusades 117

D

Der Meistertrunk 2, 8, 9, 12, 13, 22, 24, 36, 39, 40, 57, 96
Detwang 5, 10, 18, 28, 29, 50, 52, 86, 87, 110, 120, 121
Deutscher Ritterorden 5, 10, 36, 50, 120
Deutschherrngasse 76
Deutschvölkischer Schutz- und Trutzbund 90
Dinkelsbühl 116, 117
Domdey, Ingo 17, 75
Doppelbrücke 13, 27, 29, 114, 115, 123
Dornfelder 112
Dubron 112
Dürer, Albrecht 52
Dürerhaus Grafikmuseum 14, 17, 25, 75

E

Edition Rothenburger Series 75
Eiswiese 29, 113

Emperor Friedrich I Barbarossa 10, 94
Emperor Friedrich II 5
Emperor Karl IV 65, 119
Emperor Ludwig the Bavarian 106
Emperor Maximilian I 42
Engelsburg 29, 122
Erlbacher Straße 18, 115
Essigkrug 5, 10, 87
Eulschirbenmühle 111
Evangelische Tagungsstätte 28, 110, 111

F

Faulturm 59, 70, 99
Feuchtwangen 117
Fleisch- und Tanzhaus 16, 48, 49, 56
Flürlein, Kaspar 38
Förderverein Taubermühlenweg e.V. 110
Franciscan Church 10, 17, 84
Franciscan monastery 85
Franconia 2, 8, 21, 48, 90, 91
Franconian cuisine 20
Frankenhöhe 114, 119
Franken-Therme 15
Frankfurt 29, 114
Fränkisches Freilandmuseum 15
Frauenturm 59
Frühlingserwachen 22
Fuchsmühle 110
Fürbringerturm 62
Füssen 100, 116

G

Gackstatter, Hans 98
Galgengasse 58, 65, 74, 75
Galgentor 10, 41, 62, 64, 65, 67
Galgenturm 60
Gebsattel 11, 117
Gebsattel Castle 90
Gebsattel, Konstantin Freiherr von 90
Gebsattlertor 65
Georgengasse 5, 74, 75
Gerlach, Georg 69
Gerlachschmiede 69
Goethe-Institut 13, 85
Göggingen 110
Graf Burkhard 87
Grafenburg 87
Grafen von Komburg 5, 87
Graf Otto von Flügelau 102, 103

Graf von Gamburg 111
Graf von Komburg 10
Graf von Tilly, Johann 7, 12, 36, 39, 40, 59, 60
Großer Stern 101
Günzburg 100

H

Hafengasse 37, 70
Hans Sachs Spiele 45
Hegereiterhaus 102, 104
Heidelberg 62, 116
Heideloff, Karl Alexander von 51
Heilig-Blut-Altar 12, 16, 24, 50, 53, 120
Heilig-Blut-Kapelle 11, 50
Heilig-Blut-Reliquie 10, 16, 25, 50, 52, 53
Heilig-Kreuz-Altar 18, 29, 120
Henkersturm 62
Heringsbronnengässchen 89
Herlin, Friedrich 12, 13, 16, 25, 50, 52
Herrngasse 8, 17, 26, 36, 37, 38, 54, 66, 82, 83,
    84, 85, 87, 89, 115
Hessing, Friedrich 110
Hessingstrasse 28
Heterichsbrunnen 22, 24, 44, 45, 48
Hirsching, Michael 43
Historiengewölbe 16, 24, 39, 46, 47, 98
Hitler, Adolf 8, 13, 37, 66, 90, 114
Hitler Youth 110
Hof 70
Hofer Schnitz 21
Hofmann 99
Hohenlohe, Albrecht von 94
Holy Roman Empire 72
Hörber, Adam 41
Hornburgweg 63, 109
Hundsturm 107
Hus, Jan 70
Hussite War 58, 70, 71

I

Imperial Castle 5, 6, 10, 17, 36, 73, 86, 87, 90
Imperial City 1, 6, 10, 24, 29, 37, 38, 42, 46,
    50, 52, 61, 62, 68, 74, 87, 97, 106
Imperial Eagle 24, 38, 40, 65, 86, 97, 107, 108
Imperial Hall 40
Imperial Ministeriales 1, 82, 87
Inner Council 7, 38, 42, 43, 46, 47, 48, 53, 54,
    55, 58, 59, 65, 68, 70, 77, 82, 85, 94,
    95, 106, 108, 109, 118, 122

J

Jagstheimerhaus 42
Jakobswanderweg 51, 101
Jewish community 6, 8, 11, 12, 13, 25, 56, 72,
74, 76, 77, 89, 91, 118
Jewish dance house 74
Johannitertor 98
Judengasse 11, 25, 58, 73, 76, 77, 85, 86

K

Kalkturm 114
Kapellenplatz 72, 73
Kappenzipfel 5, 6, 11, 12, 27, 51, 98, 99, 100,
102, 107, 108, 109, 120
Karlstadt, Andreas 116
Käthe-Wohlfahrts-Weihnachtsland 16, 49
King Albrecht I 11, 100
King Friedrich II 87
King Konrad III 5, 10, 86, 88
King Ludwig IX 73
King Maximilian I 74
King Maximilian II 116
King Rudolf I 6, 61, 84
King Wenzel 11, 90, 118, 119
Kirchner, Emil 8, 96
Kleiner Stern 101
Kletterwald Rothenburg 3, 14, 29, 122, 123
Klingengasse 50
Klingentor 10, 17, 24, 25, 29, 44, 58, 59, 60,
61, 62, 104, 111
Klingenturm 60
Klostergarten 16, 25, 54, 55
Klosterweth 25, 58, 109
Knoblauchsland 20
Köbler 122
Kobolzeller Kapelle 10, 29, 87, 116, 117
Kobolzeller Steige 29, 100, 114
Kobolzeller Tor 96, 97, 114
Kohlturm 97
Köln 82
Komburg 87
Köpfleinswiese 64, 65
Körner, Christoph 44
Kristallnacht 8, 13, 91
Kummereck 59, 61, 62
Kurzer Steig 29, 111

L

Landhege 6, 11, 118
Landwehr 1, 5, 6, 7, 8, 11, 12, 13, 14, 27, 29,
36, 41, 42, 44, 46, 47, 48, 50, 56, 61,
67, 70, 72, 74, 76, 77, 82, 88, 94, 99,
101, 106, 118, 122, 123
Leprosyium 117
Leuzenbronner Straße 29, 122, 123
Leyk's Lotos Garten 18, 115
Libavius, Andreas 16, 46
Lichtel 118
Liebliches Taubertal 119
Lübeck 82
Luther, Martin 7, 48, 84

M

Magdeburg 40
Magnus, Albertus 54
Maktplatz 60
Mannheim 116
Maria-Krönungs-Altar 25, 52
Markgraf Casimir von Ansbach 48, 49
Marktplatz 6, 7, 8, 9, 12, 15, 22, 23, 24, 26, 27,
36, 37, 39, 42, 45, 49, 70, 82, 86, 108,
114, 118
Markusturm 5, 36, 70, 71, 86
McCloy, John 8, 67
Medical doctors 109
Melusine 111
Mergentheim 67
Merian the Elder, Matthäus 13, 29, 122, 123
Merovingian dynasty 5
Michaelskapelle 29, 52, 120
Midwives 109
Milchmarkt 71, 72
Mindelheim 100
Mittelalterliche Kriminalmuseum 2, 3, 11, 18,
26, 27, 55, 92, 93, 98
Montgelas, Maximilian Graf von 75
Müller-Thurgau 112
Munich 62, 74

N

Napoleon 8, 74, 77
Nazi regime 8, 29, 66, 74, 110, 114, 115
Neue Spital 6, 9, 11, 27, 51, 87, 98, 100, 101,
102, 103, 104, 105, 106, 117
Neusitz 54

Nordenberg, Lupold von 54, 71, 87
Nördlingen 1, 67, 116
NSDAP Rothenburg Stadt 90
Nürnberg 1, 6, 11, 20, 21, 29, 36, 38, 45, 47,
    61, 82, 90, 91, 92, 93, 100, 106, 114,
    116, 119
Nusch, Georg 7, 39, 40

O

Obere Schmiedgasse 27, 42, 43, 49, 118
Oertel, Johannes 37
Ohmayer, Alfons 66
Ohrbach 49
Order of Augustinians 102
Order of Benedictines 87
Order of Dominicans 5, 9, 10, 13, 16, 17, 25,
    36, 54, 55, 56, 84, 85, 87
Order of Franciscans 5, 11, 12, 17, 25, 26, 36,
    54, 57, 84, 85
Order of St John 5, 10, 11, 18, 27, 36, 84, 92,
    94, 95, 97, 100, 101, 102, 105
Otnat, Michael 45
Outer Council 12, 46, 63

P

Paris 73
Passau 102
Peace of Mergentheim 6
Peasants' Revolt 7, 12, 37, 43, 48, 84, 116
Pfäffleinsbad 108
Pfeifersgäßchen 70
pharmacists 108
Piccolomini, Octavio 12
Plönlein 26, 27, 96, 97, 113
Pope Francis 13, 85
Pope Martin V 70
Prague Defenestration 60
Pulverturm 62

R

Rabbi Baruch, Meir ben 10, 73
Ratskeller 7, 24, 36, 37, 40, 44
Reformation 7, 12, 16, 29, 51, 54, 55, 56, 77,
    84, 94, 95
Regensburg 1
Reichardsroth 10, 94
Reichsarchiv München 71
Reichsdeputationshauptschluss 13
Reichshofstatt 46

Reichsschultheiß Lupoid von Weitingen 102
Reichsstadt-Festtage 22, 36, 41, 45, 82
Reichsstadthalle 9, 102, 104, 106, 107
Reichstag 119
Reiterle 23, 36, 83
Richter, Ludwig 3
Riehl, Wilhelm Heinrich 2
Riemenschneider, Tilman 3, 12, 16, 18, 24,
    25, 28, 29, 50, 52, 53, 84, 120
Rintfleisch Pogrom 6, 11, 73, 90, 91
Röderbogen 5, 10, 25, 70, 71
Rödergasse 58, 66, 67, 70, 71
Röderschütt 27
Rödertor 10, 55, 63, 67, 69, 77
Röderturm 8, 17, 27, 60, 63, 66, 67
Romantische Straße 2, 116
Romanze an Valentin 23
Rosenthal, Toby 96
Rossmühle 12, 27, 63, 100, 102, 104, 105
Rostbratwurst 21
Rothenburg-Blick 122
Rothenburger Hans Sachs Spiele 23
Rothenburger Herbstmesse 23
Rothenburger Künstlerbund e.V. 16, 49
Rothenburger Märchenzauber 23, 83
Rothenburger Neue Wasserkunst 111
Rothenburger Passion 12, 17, 24, 25, 56,
    57, 84
Rothenburger Ski Jump 3, 29, 122
Rothenburger Volksfest 22
Rothenburger Weindorf 22
Rothenburg Museum 3, 5, 9, 10, 12, 13, 17,
    23, 24, 25, 36, 41, 43, 45, 54, 56, 57,
    59, 73, 76, 77, 84
Rothenburg Tourism Service 40
Röttingen 91
Ruckesser 99, 101, 109

S

Sachs, Hans 45
Saint Francis of Assisi 84
Saint George 24, 44
Saint Jacob 50, 52
Saint Leonhard 117
Saint Rochus 60
Saint Sebastian 60
Saint Wolfgang 44, 60
Salzburg 8, 84
Sammlung Baumann 56, 57
Saurer Zipfel 21

Sausteige 107
Schandtauber 101, 112
Schäufele 21
Schillingsfürst 88, 117
Schletterer, Theodor 45
Schmalkaldian War 12
Schmid, Johannes 84
Schneeballen 3, 15, 20
Schneiderstürmle 86
Schöngras 101
Schrannenplatz 6, 55, 76, 77
Schulz-Leyk, Bernd 18, 115
Schwabenmühle 28, 110
Schwäbisch Gmünd 1
Schwäbisch Hall 84
Schwarz, Martinus 57
Schwarzriesling 112
Schwetzingen 116
Seckendorf, Ursula von 59
Second City War 71
Seelenbrunnen 72, 73
Servi camerae regis 72
Shepherd's Dance 22, 36
Siebersturm 27, 96, 98, 99, 100
Silvaner 112
Sommer, Hans 111
Spitalbastei 110
Spitalgasse 98, 101, 102, 103, 109
Spitalkirche Rothenburg 103
Spitaltor 27, 28, 100, 101, 102, 108, 109, 117
Spitalviertel 105
Spitzweg, Carl 3, 8, 13, 95, 96
Staufer dynasty 1, 5, 11, 17, 26, 36, 68, 81, 82, 86, 87, 88
Steinach 118
Sterngasse 99
Sterntürme 70
St Jakob 2, 6, 11, 12, 16, 24, 25, 29, 50, 51, 52, 53, 55, 71, 120, 122
St Johannis 18, 27, 94
Stöberleinsbühne 15, 27, 101, 104, 105
Stöberleinsturm 105, 107
St Peter und Paul 5, 10, 18, 28, 29, 50, 52, 120
Strafturm 59, 109
Streicher, Julius 90
St Wolfgang 12, 17, 25, 44, 45, 58, 60, 61, 63
St Wolfgang's Day 44
Sulzbach 70
Swabian Confederation 48

T

Talmud Torah 72
Tauberbischofsheim 111, 116, 119
Tauberfranken 112
Taubermühlen 118
Taubermühlenweg 110, 111
Tauber River 2, 8, 27, 28, 29, 44, 58, 73, 87, 96, 104, 111, 112, 113, 114, 116, 120
Tauberschwarz 112
Taubertal Festival 22, 29, 113
Taubertalweg 110, 111, 118
Tauber Valley 2, 3, 5, 6, 8, 10, 14, 17, 18, 26, 27, 28, 29, 36, 50, 51, 58, 67, 81, 86, 88, 90, 91, 96, 97, 98, 100, 101, 110, 112, 119, 120, 123
Teuschlein, Johannes 77, 84
Thirty Years' War 1, 2, 7, 8, 12, 16, 22, 24, 36, 37, 40, 46, 47, 58, 60, 62, 64, 67, 74, 82, 96
Thüringen 120
Topographia Germaniae 122
Toppler, Heinrich 6, 11, 16, 18, 24, 28, 29, 38, 39, 42, 46, 47, 50, 76, 83, 88, 95, 118, 119, 123
Topplerschlösschen 3, 11, 18, 28, 29, 118, 119
Toppler Theater 15, 23, 45
Totenweth 55
tourism industry 83, 88, 96, 97
town hall 3, 6, 10, 11, 12, 16, 24, 26, 29, 36, 37, 38, 39, 40, 41, 42, 46, 48, 52, 60, 71, 82, 119, 122
Treuchtlingen 15
Tübingen 39, 109
Turenne, Graf Henri de (französischer General) 12
Turenne, Henri de 12

U

Ulm 1
Unbehaben, Ernst 39

V

Verein Alt-Rothenburg 27, 56, 66
Vienna 67
vineyards 14

W

Wasse, Arthur 57

Weidmann, Leonhard 38, 53
Weikersheim 119
Weinsteige 29
Weißer Turm 5, 25, 66, 72, 74, 75, 86
Wertheim 112, 119
Wettringen 112, 118
Weyden, Rogier van der 52
Wildbad 8, 13, 15, 28, 96, 110, 114, 115
winemaker 112
Winterglühen 23
witch hunt 98
Wittenberg 7, 48
Wochenmarkt 23
World War I 6, 66, 90, 110
World War II 1, 6, 8, 9, 17, 27, 53, 54, 63, 66,
        67, 68, 69, 74, 76, 90, 110
Worms 73
Würzburg 6, 11, 29, 36, 47, 61, 64, 71, 73, 91,
        94, 98, 102, 112, 116, 117, 119, 120

Y

youth hostel 27, 104, 105

Z

Zehntscheune 9
Zwölf-Boten-Altar 12, 16, 25, 50, 52

The Author

Rudolf is a widely travelled cosmopolitan. He was born in Munich, graduated in physics with distinction at the Ludwig-Maximilians Universität and completed his doctorate on star formation at the Max Planck Institute for Astrophysics. He then followed the call to become a senior management consultant in London, where he advised the leaders of the financial services industry for nearly ten years. His passion for the Tango tempted him to Buenos Aires. There, he studied psychology and sociology at the Universidad de Palermo. Rudolf is drawn to the analytical school of Carl Gustav Jung. His travels across the globe carried him to the Middle East, to Asia and Africa; in Latin America, he feels at home. The globetrotter speaks three languages fluently, and he is convinced that the tongue of the heart is the most important one. Rudolf is a passionate photographer and never at a loss for a story.

The Book

Rothenburg ob der Tauber: Strictly Confidential is more than just an ordinary travel guide. It describes a journey through town to discover the culturally rich city in 41 travel points with the eyes of a local. The author presents Rothenburg's historical background in an engaging and informative manner; from emotional experience and intuitive understanding to hard facts, the book provides never-ending insight into Rothenburg and the life of its burghers. The focus is not on individual sights, but the author delves into the historical development of the city. "It is only when we look at the whole," says Rudolf, "that the detail makes sense." Just flipping through the pages enthrals to adventure. With the guide *Rothenburg ob der Tauber: Strictly Confidential*, the world-traveller feels the excitement of exploring the cultures of this marvellous blue planet called home to all earthlings.

Rudolf H. Stehle

ROTHENBURG
OB DER TAUBER

PHEKARUMA TRAVEL GUIDE

Phekaruma is an indie project that aims to enrich the niche market of culturally interested globetrotters using cutting-edge PoD technologies.

Since the turn of the millennium, the psychological energy of globalization has overshadowed that of nationalistic trends. The conflict between regional and global dynamics defines our time. In the chain of ancestry, the task of the 21st century is to bring the world's cultures together without reducing them to the lowest common denominator. Diversity in unity is only achieved through understanding and through emotional openness. The Phekaruma Travel Guides want to help outgrow this challenge.